LEONARD R. BRAND & RICHARD M. DAVIDSON

100 MILLION YEARS

D1522850

Choose You This Day

Why It Matters
What You Believe
About Creation

Pacific Press®
Publishing Association

Nampa, Idaho | Oshawa, Ontario, Canada
www.pacificpress.com

Cover design by Steve Lanto

Cover design resources from Leonard Brand, who assumes all responsibilities for securing art rights.

Inside design by Kristin Hansen-Mellish

Copyright © 2013 by Pacific Press® Publishing Association

Printed in the United States of America

All rights reserved

You can obtain additional copies of this book by calling toll-free 1-800-765-6955 or by visiting http://www.adventistbookcenter.com.

ISBN 13: 978-0-8163-4434-5
ISBN 10: 0-8163-4434-5

13 14 15 16 17 • 5 4 3 2 1

DEDICATION

Dedicated to all who are seeking to
know the truth about our Creator.

TABLE OF CONTENTS

PREFACE

Two friends examined a group of fossil trees in Wyoming, pondered their meaning—and arrived at diametrically opposed conclusions! Both were trained scientists. They carefully used the methods of geological research to understand the fossil trees. One decided the evidence he gathered from those fossil trees meant the biblical story of Creation and subsequent earth history was a myth. The other considered what the Bible says about the origin of this world to be reliable. So he took the apparent contradiction between the Bible and the current geological interpretation as a call for more study of the geological facts. He did the research, and his findings were accepted for publication in a scientific journal.

How can the same information lead two people to such differing conclusions? How can we avoid being misled?

This is not another book containing analyses of the various evidences for creation and evolution. Rather, we intend it to focus people's attention on why what we believe about creation is important. Why it matters. What does belief in a literal, seven-day Creation week have to do with the gospel of Jesus Christ? Is it really important?

As we pursue those questions, we'll weave into our presentation just enough evidence to illustrate how to think about the Bible and science and what priorities to set. What is the role of the divine, revealed Word, and what is the role of the human search for understanding? After all, it was God who gave us minds, and He's the One who gave us the Bible. We can use both if we keep the right perspectives.

We puzzle over why there is so much evil in this world. Why are we surrounded by murder, lies, theft, disease, pain, and the death of people we love? Why is our world plagued by agony-causing earthquakes, volcanoes, tsunamis, and floods? We can't find answers to our questions about creation and about who God is without understanding evil.

The Christian portion of the scholarly world is rapidly separating into two groups. One group makes evolutionary science their standard and accepts theistic evolution (also called *evolutionary creationism*)—the belief that the world and life on it has existed for millions of years and that evolution was God's means of creating life-forms. The other group considers the Bible to be God's revelation, and they believe its accounts of a literal, seven-day Creation week and a global flood to be true. We maintain that the second position is the right one—in fact, that it's the only one that reflects the glory, infinite wisdom, and Personhood of God.

Some details of how we talk about this issue are more important than a cursory look at them may suggest, because some people redefine terms to suit their purposes and do so without revealing what they mean by what they say. They may, for instance, say that they believe in creation, or even in a Bible-based version of creation, thus apparently revealing where they stand on the issue. However, many theistic evolutionists think that people can believe in the biblical story of Creation while also believing that the process God used to create this world was the theistic form of evolution, and that creation took long ages of time. So, we know that people really mean they believe in the biblical Creation only if they specify what that includes: a literal, seven-day Creation week that took place a few thousand years ago.

The presentation in this book is the result of several decades of study and regular meetings with groups focused on the issues of faith and science, creation and evolution, and geology. It also reflects four decades of field and laboratory research in geology and paleontology by one of the authors, and nearly four decades of Old Testament study by the other author, with both of us thinking of how to integrate faith and science.

We don't expect that everyone will agree with what we have written. But we invite you to consider carefully the point of view presented here, and, if you think we are wrong, to show us the evidence.

We are indebted to our colleagues for the thought-provoking ideas they bring to us. We are indebted to our students for challenging us to continue to improve the answers we give in response to their questions. And we are indebted to those who disagree with us. They provoke us to dig deeper into our subject matter.

We received valuable critiques of the original manuscript from John Baldwin, Art Chadwick, David Cowles, Joe Galusha, Tom Goodwin, Clifford Goldstein, and Ed Zinke. Their suggestions have resulted in many improvements. We, the authors, are responsible for the concepts presented here and for any remaining errors.

CHAPTER 1

THE CHALLENGE

Throughout history, the Christian understanding of the Bible has suffered a series of challenges from the sciences. Even now—especially now—human beings are saying their theories call into question the reliability, the trustworthiness of the divine Word of God. Why does this happen? The answer can teach us important lessons about trust, patience, human science, and our relationship to Jesus.

With his theory of an earth that turns on its axis and revolves around the sun, Copernicus disturbed the long-accepted geocentric view of the universe. After Copernicus's death, Galileo ended up under house arrest for advocating Copernicus's novel idea, which didn't square with the beliefs of the church. Later, Darwin shook up the Christian world even more with his claims that species aren't fixed but evolve through the ages. Add to that the claims that Genesis contains two conflicting Creation accounts and that Moses had wrongly believed that the universe was like an upside-down metal bowl that rested on a flat earth and held the stars up in the sky. And then there was the claim in Joshua 10:13 that God disturbed the movement of the sun just so the Israelites could win a battle. How could people believe stories like these when the heavenly orbits are so clearly consistent and reliable? (See page 86 of this book for a further comment on this story.)

Now, in the twenty-first century, we are faced with more challenges: bold assertions of radiometric dating that is trustworthy and that demonstrates that the earth has existed for many millions of years, of ice cores containing tens of thousands of annual layers, of a fossil record that clearly shows the evolution of life-forms, and of archaeological evidence that reveals that the biblical Exodus didn't happen—at least not the way the Bible describes it.

This long series of conflicts between the Bible and science has shaken the confidence of many in the reliability of Scripture. Can we trust its message about history? And if its claims about history aren't factual, what about its claims about a time when the earth will be made new?

The scholarly Christian world is rapidly coming to a consensus that the story of a literal creation and a worldwide flood a few thousand years ago is only a myth. Instead, many now believe that life has evolved through the millennia. The corollary to this view is that evil didn't result from Adam and Eve's sin; it was just a natural part of evolution. Is this shift of belief inevitable, or have we missed something?

Central to this issue is the relationship between faith and science—particularly, how we handle conflicts between science and the Bible without either pushing God out of the way or diminishing the positive insights that science has brought to us. In the following pages, we present an answer to these challenges that is faithful to the Bible.

The challenge in perspective: Cosmic conflict

Have you ever noticed how many books, movies, and cartoons are based on the theme of an epic battle between good and evil? The stories told by these media generally feature a good guy or two and their valiant efforts to thwart the evil witch, the cattle rustler, or the cosmic forces that are trying to force evil plans on the universe. Why this fascination with stories of bitter conflict between evil and the heroism of the defenders of all things good? Could it be that these modern tales reflect the original cosmic conflict—the great controversy between Christ and Satan? That story is the essential platform for understanding the story of Creation and its challengers, and that's why it matters whether we believe it.[1]

An extensive study of the Bible confirms that this story of the great controversy between Christ and Satan and the accompanying message of salvation through Jesus is its central issue.[2] Christianity is not based on abstract theory but on a series of events that occurred in history.

God created the universe sinless and without evil, pain, or death. It was a place of beauty and harmony, and the universal acceptance of God's law resulted in universal peace and happiness. But when He created human beings, He made a tough decision. He could have created them as robots that would never disobey, but then their obedience would never be motivated by love for their Creator. So, rather than making the angels and later the humans to be obedient robots, God instead gave them the gift of <u>free will</u>. And He did so even though He knew the terrible price He would have to pay if we rebelled.

Eventually, of course, Lucifer, the angel who held the highest position in God's government, did rebel, and consequently he became Satan. Then he influenced Adam and Eve to join his rebellion, exposing the earth and human beings to his power and the evil he has brought upon us. But we not only suffer from evil, we commit it as well. Satan successfully tempts us to commit moral evils, including theft and murder—both of which grow out of selfishness.

Why can't we think our way out of this dilemma and reject Satan's schemes?

Because he's much too intelligent and too strong for us—unless we depend on God's continual presence and power and the guidance His Word provides. Satan's cleverness and deceptive ways are legendary, and he is quite willing to use one weapon God will never use—lies. His continual, wily use of lies is one reason for his success.

We can grasp this only if we accept the biblical view that God and Satan aren't impersonal forces, but rather are personal beings—One who loves us and desires our happiness, and one who hates us and seeks to destroy us.

Because our sins are the source of all this trouble, we need a Redeemer. Jesus took upon Himself this role, living and dying on earth to defeat Satan's plan to grasp control of the universe. The resurrected Jesus provides the ultimate gift: salvation and eternal life, which we will receive in a re-created world where there will no longer be any sin or evil. The great controversy is the story of how sin began and how Christ will end it.[3]

We will return to this story and examine how it affects the issues we encounter in the relationship between faith and science.

ENDNOTES

1. See J. Eldredge, *Epic: The Story God Is Telling* (Nashville: Thomas Nelson, 2004).

2. E. G. White, *The Great Controversy Between Christ and Satan* (Mountain View, Calif.: Pacific Press® Publishing Association, 1950); R. M. Davidson, "Cosmic Metanarrative for the Coming Millennium," *Journal of the Adventist Theological Society* 11, nos. 1, 2 (Spring–Autumn 2000): 102–119.

3. White, *The Great Controversy*.

Chapter 2

Resolving the Conflicts

Scientists explore the earth and the universe, and their interpretations of their discoveries at times pose challenges to the Bible. In the previous chapter, we listed some of those challenges. Now, our question is how we should address the questions those challenges raise. We can allow them to destroy our faith in Scripture and inevitably then in the God of Scripture, or we can seek divine guidance in our search for answers. God invites us to taste and see that He is trustworthy. We're convinced that because the Bible was inspired by the infinite God of the universe, we don't have to fear that honest investigation will disprove it.

The Bible is the standard against which all the elements of our belief system must be assessed. "A sense of the power and wisdom of God, and of our inability to comprehend His greatness, should inspire us with humility, and we should open His Word, as we would enter His presence, with holy awe. When we come to the Bible, reason must acknowledge an authority superior to itself, and heart and intellect must bow before the great I AM."[1]

To be truly Christian, one's worldview must consider the Bible to be trustworthy—a sound basis for an integrated view of the world. A Christian worldview must, then, offer a "biblically informed perspective on all reality"[2] that doesn't separate religion from the rest of experience and knowledge.

With that view of the Bible in mind, we suggest that careful study of science, the Bible, and the historical and sociological context of the conflicts between them can bring greater clarity to our understanding of the conflicts and help us resolve them. We won't always be able to understand the issues clearly right away; sometimes understanding will come only after time and study provide a better perspective.

Galileo

Galileo's story is often cited as exhibit A of the case against allowing the Bible to influence our understanding of science. Those who argue for the primacy of science say his story shows the necessity of allowing science to correct theologically biased ideas about nature.

During Galileo's lifetime, the geocentric theory, which claimed that the sun orbits around the earth rather than the earth around the sun, was standard science and also orthodox Christian belief. And some statements in the Bible appeared to support the geocentric theory. They seemed to say that it is the sun that moves; the earth stands still.[3] For instance, Psalm 19:6 and Ecclesiastes 1:5 speak of the sun rising and moving across the sky.

Because of the church dogmas associated with these texts, it may have been difficult for the participants in this drama to see them clearly. We, who live long after Galileo, have the benefit of hindsight,[4] along with much more knowledge of both the relevant science and the historical and biblical context. And though we know the truth of the matter—that it is the earth that moves and the sun that stands still—we use the same expressions, saying that the sun rises and sets. We know that the sun doesn't actually move in relation to us. We use these expressions because they fit what we see.[5] It seems the biblical writers were using expressions similar to ours in the same way we use ours.

Other Bible texts speak of the earth as established, saying it won't move. But we don't find these texts in biblical essays on cosmology; they're in chapters whose themes are the greatness or majesty of God and the value of His laws (1 Chronicles 16:30; Psalms 93; 104; 119), not the facts of cosmology. The descriptive statements about the earth are incidental to the themes of the chapters.

Before Copernicus and Galileo, there was no reason to wonder whether these verses were making a scientific claim about the heavens or just describing how things looked from our position on earth. Before Copernicus, both cosmology and the Bible seemed to agree that the earth stood still. However, when we view these Bible texts in their immediate context, we recognize that they aren't scientific statements, but simply describe what appears to be the case in the same way we do today.

The geocentric theory, in fact, came from Greek science

and philosophy, not from a deep understanding of the Bible.[6] In contrast to Genesis 1, Bible texts such as Psalm 19:6 and Ecclesiastes 1:5 are not meant to be descriptive accounts of creation. In fact, the church's treatment of Galileo was motivated more by disputes within science, by church politics that was putting pressure on Pope Urban III, and by Galileo's own abrasive personality than by conflict between science and the church. Other astronomers of that time discussed the heliocentric theory without suffering Galileo's fate.[7] One historian calls the idea that the Catholic Church condemned Galileo "for having discovered the truth" one of the most common myths about the Galileo affair. He says some people use this myth "to justify the incompatibility between science and religion," and he concludes that "this thesis is erroneous, misleading, and simplistic."[8]

That episode alerts us to the dangers of basing our interpretation of Scripture on current scientific beliefs, as the church did in the pre-Galileo era. We can now see that science really did improve our understanding of the Bible because it showed the errors of Greek cosmology that were being read *into* the Bible and that because of them people were suggesting untenable interpretations of texts they didn't understand. It also encourages us to respond to apparent conflicts between science and Scripture with careful study so that we don't make the same mistake people made then: reading into the Bible things that actually aren't there. We'll address examples of that faulty practice later. Right now, let's outline the direction of our current discussion.

We suggest there are three stages in our coming to understand the Galileo affair:

Stage 1:   Conflict and confusion
Stage 2:   Research in science, deep Bible study, and the additional perspective that hindsight provides
Stage 3:   Resolution and insight

The diagram below fills out further the three-stage process, picturing a constructive approach to the integration of religion and science, both of which are thus grounded in a biblical worldview.[9]

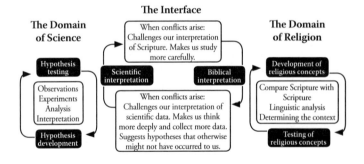

In the process represented in this diagram, science doesn't test religious concepts nor does the latter test the former. But science and religion aren't isolated from each other either. Instead, conflicts between them are analyzed in the thinking process called the "Interface."[10] Seeming conflicts between Scripture and science challenge us to a more careful study of *both* as we seek a resolution to the conflict. The help that hindsight provides toward resolving the conflict comes from the Interface thinking process.

To resolve conflicts involving science and religion using the previous diagram, we move from conflict (stage 1) through research (stage 2), to resolution (stage 3) in a thoughtful interfacing of scientific and biblical interpretations. However, we must realize that we don't know all there is to be known about interpreting what we see either in science or the Bible. We must realize that, in some cases, the facts necessary to removing the conflicts may not have been discovered yet. If that's the case, we may have to wait a long time—maybe longer than we have—for the resolution of those conflicts.

The same Creator God made both the universe and the Book that tells us about it, but we don't adequately understand either. The method of study described here enables us to examine authoritatively both sources of evidence.

Endnotes

1. E. G. White, *Steps to Christ* (Mountain View, Calif.: Pacific Press®, 1956), 110.
2. N. Pearcey, *Total Truth: Liberating Christianity From Its Cultural Captivity* (Wheaton, Ill.: Crossway Books, 2005), 23.
3. M. Finocchiaro, *The Galileo Affair: A Documentary History* (Berkeley, Calif.: University of California Press, 1989).

4. "Hindsight" is not included here as a hermeneutical principle. Rather, we think of it as a simple reminder that, in some cases, time must pass before the portion of Scripture and/or science in question is understood well enough to allow us to resolve the conflict. In other words, patience—and faith—are necessary.

5. The sun does move with the rest of our galaxy, but that doesn't alter the issue we're addressing.

6. N. Hetherington, ed., *Encyclopedia of Cosmology: Historical, Philosophical, and Scientific Foundations of Modern Cosmology* (New York: Garland Publishing, 1993).

7. J. Gribbin, *Science: A History* (New York: Penguin Books, 2002); M. Dorn, *Das Problem der Autonomie der Naturwissenschaften bei Galilei* (Stuttgart: Steiner Verlag, 2000); W. Milan, "Galileo: The Strange Facts in a Famous Story," Explore Zone, August 23, 1999, http://www.Explorezone.com/columns/space/1999/august_galileo.htm (site discontinued); Finocchiaro, *The Galileo Affair*.

8. Finocchiaro, *The Galileo Affair*, 5.

9. Illustration modified from figure 6.4 in L. R. Brand, *Faith, Reason, and Earth History*, 2nd ed. (Berrien Springs, Mich.: Andrews University Press, 2009), 131; also discussed in L. Brand with D. C. Jarnes, *Beginnings* (Nampa, Idaho: Pacific Press®, 2006).

10. We aren't using *interface* in a technical sense, as it was used by Thomas Aquinas; we're seeking a revelation-based understanding.

Chapter 3

Science Helps Us Understand the Bible

The conflict between science and religion that took place in Galileo's day wasn't the only one in which science improved people's understanding of the Bible. In Darwin's time, it was commonly thought that every animal and plant species was created fixed and unchangeable. Darwin's theory challenged this concept of the fixity of species. Now, with the benefit of careful study and the perspective of hindsight that we receive when we're committed to God's Word, we see that nowhere does the Bible teach the fixity of species. Genesis just doesn't say whether species, as defined by modern science, are fixed or changeable.[1]

In chapter 2, we pointed out that the concept that the earth is the center of the universe came from Greek philosophy rather than the Bible. The idea that species are "fixed," unchangeable, is also traceable to Greek philosophy and not to the Bible. In the nineteenth century, the apparent conflict between science and religion regarding this conflict generated much confusion. But now we can see that science has improved our understanding of the Bible. It has shown that species *do* change. Though the Bible rejects large-scale evolution (e.g., the evolution of reptiles, birds, humans, etc., from a common ancestor), it doesn't proclaim the fixity of species. It doesn't say that species, such as the European barn rat, the red fox, the mockingbird, and the sycamore tree, never change.

In Darwin's day, Bible-believing scientists had already concluded that organisms do change, but they believed those changes were limited to variations and adaptations *within* created groups or created *kinds*. Even Carl Linnaeus, who is generally described as an advocate of the fixity of species, gradually came to recognize that there was evidence of change. Eventually, he came to believe change was possible not only at the level of species but perhaps even up to the level of families. Darwin apparently was unaware of the work of these scientists.[2] (Just think what the course of science could have been if Darwin and his colleagues had realized that the Bible doesn't teach that species are fixed—that instead, biological adaptation may occur within each group God created!)

Another example comes from the work of early twentieth-century creationist George McCready Price. He rejected geologists' claims regarding glaciations and geological "overthrusts"—the name geologists have given to the phenomenon of mountain-sized masses of rocks being thrust on top of younger rocks. Price didn't think such massive geological events were consistent with the biblical story of Creation.[3] When he rejected these concepts, he didn't have access to sufficient information to resolve what he saw as a conflict. Now, with the benefit of more research and hindsight, we recognize that the Bible doesn't speak to these issues at all, so Price's response came not from the Bible but from his own limited understanding. Scientific research has helped us recognize that overthrusts and glaciation more extensive than we see today did exist in the past. We no longer find the idea of a global geological catastrophe that results in mountain-sized overthrusts and episodes of unbalanced, glacial climate to be impossible or unbiblical. In other words, there never really was a genuine conflict between science and the Bible about these ideas.

So science has helped us rid ourselves of ideas that had mistakenly been thought to have come from the Bible when they actually had originated elsewhere (e.g., in Greek philosophy). Heliocentrism, speciation, glaciations, and geological overthrusts don't do away with the biblical themes of the great controversy and salvation history. The claims of science about these geological processes are generally realistic and don't contradict the Bible.[4] These issues have gone through stages 1 and 2 of the diagram in chapter 2 and are now in stage 3—resolution.

Eliminating false conflicts

Genesis 1 and 2 are often portrayed as raising doubt about the veracity of Genesis because they supposedly contradict each other regarding the sequence of events during Creation.

Genesis 1 says plants were created before humans, but Genesis 2 seems to indicate that the humans were created first. This disagreement is frequently given as a reason why we shouldn't think the biblical Creation accounts were meant to be taken as literal accounts of the origin of the universe and its inhabitants. However, careful study of the Hebrew text reveals that the two Creation accounts are not in conflict; they are complementary.[5] It shows that Genesis 1 pictures the general creation of plants, and Genesis 2 portrays the somewhat later origin of agricultural plants. Thus, there is no conflict between the sequences of events in Genesis 1 and 2.

It has often been claimed that from the beginning of Christianity through the Middle Ages, Christians believed the earth was flat. But historical research has now shown that this idea is not true. While a couple of minor Christian writers did suggest that the earth is flat, few believed them. In fact, along with other scientists, most Christian scholars down through the ages knew that the earth is round and never did believe in a flat earth.[6] The idea that Christians had advocated the flat-earth theory was invented by some nineteenth-century scholars, probably in an attempt to discredit Christianity. Their inaccurate suggestion, then, became widely and uncritically accepted.

Another frequently heard claim is that the cosmology underlying the Old Testament pictures the sky as an inverted metal bowl that rests on a flat earth and holds the stars in place. But research has shown that the Old Testament doesn't picture a solid, hemispherical dome or vault that rests on a flat disc that is the earth. Those who believe it does contain that picture base their interpretation upon a faulty translation of the Babylonian term *raqia'*, from which the Hebrew concept was allegedly borrowed in the first place.

Second, it is now evident that the Mesopotamians didn't have this concept of a solid heavenly vault, and the Hebrew term in Genesis 1 that several English versions translate as "firmament" would be better translated as "sky" or "expanse." It doesn't refer to a solid dome. Actually, it was some nineteenth-century scholars who invented and advocated the theory that this upside-down-bowl cosmology underlies the Old Testament. Many scholars still suppose the Bible advocates this error, but it's just one more concept that has been read into the Bible.[7]

The Bible doesn't claim to be a comprehensive textbook on science and doesn't present a fully developed or systematized cosmology. But, notwithstanding common assertions to the contrary, many of the statements it makes that impinge upon issues of cosmology and the phenomena of nature reveal a remarkable reliability and precision. Old Testament passages that are in cosmological contexts may well be understood as not describing the earth as a flat disc but as spherical in shape and suspended in space rather than resting upon anything.

For instance, Isaiah says God "sits above the circle [*chug*] of the earth" (Isaiah 40:22). The Hebrew word *chug* is often translated as "circle," but "sphere" would probably be a better translation. And Job declares, "He stretches out the north[ern] [skies] over empty space; He hangs the earth on nothing [*beli mah*]" (Job 26:7, NKJV). Translated literally, the phrase *beli mah* means "without something." In other words, the translation "nothing" is justified, and Job's statement coincides with what we know about the earth. Further intensive exegetical investigation may clear up other cosmological misunderstandings.

In the cases cited in this chapter, the conflict (stage 1) didn't originate directly from science or from the Bible but from erroneous claims made by scholars that the Bible was scientifically incorrect. Research is now bringing resolution (stage 3) by showing that neither the Bible nor those who were influenced by it held the beliefs that some scholars claimed they did. Specifically, Genesis doesn't have the faults that many people have supposed it does.

ENDNOTES

1. See A. R. Schafer, "The 'Kinds' of Genesis 1: What Is the Meaning of *Mîn?*" *Journal of the Adventist Theological Society* 14, no. 1 (Spring 2003): 86–100. The results of sin Genesis 3 spoke of do indicate change.

2. P. Landgren, "On the Origin of 'Species': Ideological Roots of the Species Concept," in *Typen des Lebens,* ed. S. Scherer (Berlin: Pascal-Verlag [Studium Integrale], 1993), 47–64.

3. G. M. Price, *Illogical Geology* (Los Angeles: Modern Heretic Publications, 1906); Price, *The New Geology* (Mountain View, Calif.: Pacific Press®, 1923); H. W. Clark, *Crusader for Creation* (Mountain View, Calif.: Pacific Press®, 1966).

4. According to mainline science, some of these processes require long time periods. However, whether this is correct is not a settled matter.

5. R. Younker, *God's Creation: Exploring the Genesis Story* (Nampa, Idaho: Pacific Press®, 1999); R. Younker, "Genesis 2: A Second Creation Account?" in *Creation, Catastrophe, and Calvary,* ed. J. T. Baldwin (Hagerstown, Md.: Review and Herald® Publishing Association, 2000), 69–78; Younker, "How Can We Interpret the First Chapters of Genesis?" in *Understanding Creation,* eds. L. J. Gibson and H. Rasi (Nampa, Idaho: Pacific Press®, 2011), 69–77; J. Moskala, "A Fresh Look at Two Genesis Creation Accounts: Contradictions?" *Andrews University Seminary Studies* 49, no. 1 (Spring 2011): 45–65.

6. S. J. Gould, "The Persistently Flat Earth," *Natural History* 103 (Mar. 1994): 12, 14–19; J. B. Russell, *Inventing the Flat Earth* (Westport, Conn.: Praeger Publishers, 1997).

7. R. W. Younker and R. M. Davidson, "The Myth of the Solid Heavenly Dome: Another Look at the Hebrew רקיע (*raqia*)," *Andrews University Seminary Studies* 49, no. 1 (Spring 2011): 125–147.

CHAPTER 4

WHAT *DOES* THE BIBLE SAY ABOUT ORIGINS?

Does Genesis 1–11 really teach a recent, literal, seven-day Creation week and a global flood? We can't just decide this according to our preferences; we must depend on careful study of the original Hebrew. The following summary of the biblical evidence leads us to reply with a firm Yes to the three main parts of this question.

1. Does the Genesis account of origins describe a literal, seven-day week?

Several lines of evidence within the text of Genesis itself indicate the Creation account was intended to be taken as literal.[1] First, many scholars have shown that the literary genre Genesis 1–11 fits best is "historical narrative prose,"[2] which means it was intended to be a literal, historical account of creation. The narratives of Genesis 1 and 2 lack any clues that they are some kind of nonliteral, symbolic, metaphorical, or "metahistorical" literature.

Second, the literary structure of Genesis as a whole indicates that the creation narratives were intended to be taken as literal. It is widely recognized that the author of Genesis used the Hebrew word *toledot* ("generations," "history") in each of the thirteen sections of the book, thus revealing the book's structure. Elsewhere in Scripture, *toledot* is used in the setting of genealogies concerned with providing an accurate account of time and history. The use of *toledot* in Genesis 2:4 shows that the author intends the account of creation he is giving to be as literal as are the rest of the Genesis narratives.

Third, the author uses the phrase "evening and morning" at the conclusion of each of the six work days of Creation week to clearly define the nature of the days of Creation—they're literal, approximately twenty-four-hour-long days. Outside of Genesis 1, references to "evening" and "morning" together *invariably*—without exception in the Old Testament, where this occurs fifty-seven times—indicate a literal day.[3]

Fourth, in Genesis 1, the Hebrew word *yom,* "day," is used at the conclusion of each of the six days of Creation, and, in each case, it is used in connection with a numeric adjective ("one [first] day," "second day," "third day," etc.). This combination occurs 359 times in the rest of Scripture, and it always refers to literal days.

Fifth, the Sabbath commandment (Exodus 20:8–11) explicitly indicates that humankind's six-day workweek is the same kind of week as God's six-day workweek at Creation. Each week ends with a Sabbath, just as the Creation week did. The Divine Lawgiver unequivocally interprets the first week as a literal week that consists of seven consecutive, contiguous, literal days.

Sixth, Jesus and *all* New Testament writers refer to Genesis 1–11 with the underlying assumption that it is literal, reliable history.[4] Every chapter of this section of Genesis is referred to somewhere in the New Testament—Jesus Himself referring to Genesis chapters 1–7 as containing literal history.[5]

2. Was the Creation week recent or remote in time?

Scripture says nothing about how long ago God created the universe as a whole.[6] But there is evidence strongly implying that the Creation week described in Genesis 1:3–2:4 was recent—sometime in the last several *thousand* years; not hundreds of thousands or millions of years ago. The evidence is found primarily in the genealogies of Genesis 5 and 11. These genealogies are unique; there is nothing like them among the other genealogies of the Bible or in other ancient Near Eastern literature.[7]

Unlike the other genealogies, which may (and, in fact, often do) contain gaps, the "chronogenealogies" of Genesis 5 and 11 have indicators that they are to be taken as complete genealogies—genealogies without gaps. These unique interlocking features indicate a specific focus on chronological time and reveal an intention to make clear that there are no gaps between the individual patriarchs mentioned.

These genealogies say a patriarch lived x years and begat a son; and after he begat this son, he lived y more years and begat more sons and daughters; and all the years of this patriarch were z years. These tightly interlocking features make it virtually impossible to argue that there are significant generational gaps. Rather, they purport to present the complete time sequence from father to direct biological son throughout the genealogical sequence from Adam to Abraham. So we can conclude that it's clear that the author of the genealogies in Genesis 5 and 11 was aiming at completeness, accuracy, and precision regarding the length of time covered.[8]

There are several different textual versions of the chronological data in these two chapters: MT (the Masoretic [Hebrew] Text), LXX (the Septuagint [Greek translation] of the Old Testament), and the Samaritan Pentateuch (which is the five books of Moses). The scholarly consensus is that the MT has preserved the original figures in their purest form, while the LXX and Samaritan versions have intentionally schematized the figures for theological reasons. Even so, it's important that we recognize that though these texts differ regarding the time their genealogies cover, that difference is a matter of only about one thousand years.

Regarding the chronology from Abraham to the present, Bible-believing scholars disagree about whether the Israelite sojourn in Egypt lasted 215 years or 430 years, and thus whether to put Abraham late in the third millennium B.C. or early in the second millennium B.C. Other than this minor difference, Scripture's basic chronology from Abraham to the present is clear, and it totals about four thousand years (plus or minus two hundred years).[9]

Thus, the Bible presents a relatively recent creation of life on this earth—one that took place a few thousand years ago, not hundreds of thousands or millions or billions of years ago. While minor ambiguities don't allow us to pin down the exact date of that seven-day Creation week, based upon the biblical evidence we do have, we conclude that Scripture is perfectly clear: that week occurred *recently.*

3. Does Genesis 6–9 describe a local flood or a global flood?

Although many biblical scholars argue that Genesis 6–9 describes only a local flood, numerous lines of biblical evidence lead us to the conclusion that only a global flood does full justice to the biblical data. The major themes in Genesis 1 through 11—Creation, the Fall, the plan of redemption, and the spread of sin—are universal in scope, so they call for a matching universal judgment, which the Flood provides. Then, after the Flood, God makes a promise—a covenant. He promises there will never again be a flood like the one Noah experienced (Genesis 9:15; cf. Isaiah 54:9). God said the rainbow would be a sign to remind us of His promise (Genesis 9:9–18). If Noah's flood were only local, then every flood that has occurred since that time would break the covenant promise God made.

The ark was an enormous boat (see Genesis 6:14, 15), and the reason given for its size is that it was to save Noah, his family, and representatives of all the air-breathing terrestrial animals from the Flood by carrying them safely on the surface of the water (Genesis 6:16–21; 7:2, 3). If that flood was to be a limited one, covering only a part of the earth's surface, Noah and his family and the animals could have escaped it by simply climbing a mountain or moving to another region. The ark makes sense only as preparation for a global deluge. The Bible also says the floodwaters rose at least fifteen cubits above "all the high mountains" of the pre-Flood earth (Genesis 7:19, 20). Again, this is inconsistent with a local flood: if the water covered the highest mountains, everything else, which was all lower, would also be covered.

In addition, those who escaped the Flood were in the ark for more than a year (Genesis 7:11–8:14). That makes sense only if the Flood was global. The word *mabbul* ("flood," "deluge"), which occurs twelve times in Genesis and once in Psalms (Psalm 29:10), is reserved exclusively for reference to the Genesis Flood, thus setting that flood apart from all local floods and giving it a global context.

There are numerous other lines of biblical evidence, including more than thirty different forceful and explicitly universal expressions that are employed in the Flood narrative, that make it difficult to imagine what else the biblical writer could have done to indicate the global extent of the Genesis Flood.[10]

4. Conclusion

The conclusions we have reached regarding the biblical view of origins coincide with the findings of the vast majority of mainstream Old Testament scholars. James Barr, the late professor of Hebrew at Oxford University, summarized as follows: "So far as I know, there is no professor of Hebrew or Old Testament at any world-class university who does not believe that the writer(s) of Genesis 1–11 intended to convey to their readers the ideas that (a) creation took place in a series of six days which were the same as the days of 24 hours we now experience, (b) the figures contained in the Genesis genealogies provided by simple addition a chronology from the beginning of the world up to later stages in the biblical story, (c) Noah's flood was understood to be world-wide and [to have] extinguish[ed] all human and animal life except for those in the ark."[11]

Based upon the testimony of the Genesis account and later biblical allusions to this account, we join the host of scholars, ancient and modern, both critical and evangelical, who affirm that the Bible writer of Genesis 1–11 intended to describe a literal history of beginnings, with a literal, recent Creation week consisting of seven historical, contiguous, creative, natural (approximately twenty-four-hour) days, and a global, worldwide flood. We choose to believe that what the Bible writer recorded is an accurate history of origins.[12]

ENDNOTES

1. I (R. M. Davidson) have dealt with the major biblical issues regarding earth's origins and the extent of the Genesis Flood in more detail in several previously published articles. See esp., "In the Beginning: How to Interpret Genesis 1," *Dialogue* 6, no. 3 (1994): 9–12; and "The Biblical Account of Origins," *Journal of the Adventist Theological Society* 14, no. 1 (Spring 2003): 4–43.

These articles can be accessed on my Web site: http://www.andrews.edu/~davidson.

2. See, e.g., W. Kaiser Jr., "The Literary Form of Genesis 1–11," in *New Perspectives on the Old Testament,* ed. J. Barton Payne (Waco: Word, 1970), 48–65; cf. J. Sailhamer, *Genesis Unbound* (Sisters, Ore.: Multnomah, 1996), 227–245.

3. Even Dan. 8:14 refers to 2,300 "evening-mornings" as literal days that in Bible prophecy are to be interpreted as 2,300 years, in accordance with the "[literal] day = [literal] year" principle of prophetic interpretation that arises from within Scripture. See W. Shea, *Selected Studies on Prophetic Interpretation,* Daniel and Revelation Committee Series, vol. 1 (Washington, D.C.: Review and Herald®, 1982), where Shea gives twenty-three lines of biblical evidence for the day-year principle.

4. Matt. 19:4, 5; 23:35; 24:37–39; Mark 10:6–9; 13:19; Luke 1:70; 3:34–38; 11:50, 51; 17:26, 27; John 1:1–3, 10; 8:44; Acts 3:21; 4:25; 14:15; 17:24, 26; Rom. 1:20; 5:12, 14–19; 8:20–22; 16:20; 1 Cor. 6:16; 11:3, 7–9, 12; 15:21, 22, 38, 39, 45, 47; 2 Cor. 4:6; 11:3; Gal. 4:4, 26; Eph. 3:9; 5:30, 31; Col. 1:16; 3:10; 1 Tim. 2:13–15; Heb. 1:10; 2:7, 8; 4:3, 4, 10; 11:4, 5, 7; 12:24; James 3:9; 1 Pet. 3:20; 2 Pet. 2:4, 5; 3:4–6; 1 John 3:8, 12; Jude 6, 11, 14, 15; Rev. 2:7; 3:14; 4:11; 10:6; 12:1–4, 9, 13–17; 14:7; 17:5, 18; 20:2; 21:1, 4; 22:2, 3.

For the identification of the person or event in Gen. 1–11 indicated by these passages, see H. Morris, "Appendix B: New Testament References to Genesis 1–11," in *The Remarkable Birth of Planet Earth* (Minneapolis: Bethany Fellowship, 1972), 99–101. See also T. Mortenson, "Jesus' View of the Age of the

Earth," in *Coming to Grips With Genesis: Biblical Authority and the Age of the Earth,* eds. T. Mortenson and T. H. Ury (Green Forest, Ariz.: Master Books, 2008), 315–346; R. Minton, "Apostolic Witness to Genesis Creation and Flood," in *Coming to Grips With Genesis: Biblical Authority and the Age of the Earth,* eds. T. Mortenson and T. H. Ury (Green Forest, Ariz.: Master Books, 2008), 347–371.

Some will respond that Jesus lived in a prescientific time; and since in His human state, He didn't have access to His former divine knowledge, He didn't know the correct story of origins. However, this argument leaves God out of the equation. It also ignores one very significant fact: before Jesus came to earth, He inspired the writers who prepared the book He knew He would study during His earthly journey—the Old Testament.

5. Those who accept the inspiration of Ellen White find in her writings unambiguous testimony that Gen. 1 and 2 describe a literal week just like ours today. "I was then carried back to the creation and was shown that the first week, in which God performed the work of creation in six days and rested on the seventh day, was just like every other week. . . . God gives us the productions of his work at the close of each literal day." E. G. White, *Spiritual Gifts* (1864; repr., Washington, D.C.: Review and Herald®, 1945), 3:90.

6. The Hebrew of Gen. 1:1, 2 is open to two major interpretations, as recognized by various Seventh-day Adventist scholars. One interpretation, called the "no gap" view, sees verses 1, 2 as part of the first day of the seven-day Creation week. This interpretation

has two variations. The first variation, which may be called the "young earth, young life" view, takes the term "heavens and the earth" to apply only to this earth and its immediate surrounding heavenly spheres (the atmospheric heavens and perhaps the solar system). Thus Genesis is saying that this earth and its surrounding heavenly spheres were created recently, and according to this position, Gen. 1 says nothing about the creation of the entire universe.

The other variation of the "no gap" position may be called the "young universe, young life" view. According to this view, the term "heavens and the earth" is a merism for the entire universe. (A *merism* uses parts of the whole to refer to the whole; here, "heavens and the earth" to refer to the entire universe.) In other words, those who hold this position believe Moses was saying that the entire universe was created during the seven-day week described in Gen. 1:1–2:3. This latter position, held by some evangelicals (e.g., the Institute for Creation Research), is not regarded by most Seventh-day Adventists to be in harmony with the big picture of the great controversy, according to which unfallen intelligences (angels and inhabitants of other worlds) were in existence before the six days of Creation week described in Gen. 1 (see Job 38:4–7; Rev. 12:7–9).

The second major interpretation, commonly called the "passive gap" (or "two-stage creation") view, regards Gen. 1:1, 2 as a chronological unity separated by a gap in time from the first day of creation, which is described in verse 3. This interpretation also has two variations. According to the first variation, the expression "heavens and the earth" in verse 1 is taken as a merism referring to the entire universe, which was created "in the beginning"—before Creation week. Verse 2 describes the "raw materials" of the earth in their unformed and unfilled state, as they were created before (perhaps long before) the seven days of Creation week. Verses 3ff., then, depict the actual Creation week.

According to the second variation of the "passive gap" interpretation, the expression "heavens and the earth" refers only to this planet and its immediate surrounding heavenly spheres, which were created in their unformed and unfilled state at some point in time before the Gen. 1 Creation week. According to this variation, Gen. 1 speaks only of the creation of this world; it says nothing about the creation of the rest of the universe.

The Hebrew text seems to allow for either the "passive gap" ("two-stage creation") interpretation or the "no gap" interpretation and their variations (except for the "young universe, young life" variation of the "no gap" interpretation). This possible openness in the Hebrew text as to whether or not there is a gap between Gen. 1:1, 2 and verse 3ff., has implications for interpreting the pre-fossil layers of the geological column. If one accepts the "no gap" option, there is a possibility of relatively young pre-fossil rocks, created as part of the seven-day Creation week (perhaps with the appearance of old age). If one accepts the "passive gap" ("two-stage creation") option (my preference), there is the alternate possibility of the pre-fossil "raw materials" being created at a time of absolute beginning of this earth and its surrounding heavenly spheres at an unspecified time in the past. This initial unformed and unfilled state is described in verse

2. Verse 3 and the following verses then describe the process of forming and filling during the seven-day Creation week.

Gen. 1 leaves room for either (a) young, pre-fossil rock that was created during the seven days of creation (with the appearance of old age), or (b) older, pre-fossil earth rocks, with a long interval between the creation of these inanimate "raw materials" described in Gen. 1:1, 2 and the seven days of Creation week described in Gen. 1:3–2:3 (which I personally find the preferable interpretation). In either case, the biblical text calls for a *short* chronology for the creation of *life* on earth. According to Gen. 1, there is no room for any gap of time involving the creation of life on this earth: all earth's life-forms were created during the third through the sixth literal, contiguous, twenty-four-hour days of Creation week.

7. For other biblical genealogies, see esp. Gen. 4:16–24; 22:20–24; 25:1–4, 12–18; 29:31–30:24; 35:16–20, 22–26; 36:9–14, 40–43; 46:8–12; Ruth 4:18–22; 1 Sam. 14:50, 51; 1 Chron. 1–9; Matt. 1:1–17; and Luke 3:23–38. For comparison with nonbiblical ancient Near Eastern genealogies, see, e.g., G. F. Hasel, "The Genealogies of Gen 5 and 11 and Their Alleged Babylonian Background," *Andrews University Seminary Studies* 16 (1978): 361–374.

8. To further substantiate the absence of major gaps in the genealogies of Gen. 5 and 11, the Hebrew grammatical form of the verb "begat" (*yalad* in the *Hifil*) used throughout these chapters is the special causative form that always, elsewhere in the Old Testament, refers to actual direct physical offspring, i.e., biological father-son relationship (Gen. 6:10; Judg. 11:1;

1 Chron. 8:9; 14:3; 2 Chron. 11:21; 13:21; 24:3). This is in contrast to the use of *yalad* in the simple *Qal* form in many of the other biblical genealogies, in those cases it can refer to other than direct physical fathering of immediately succeeding offspring.

9.   See "The Chronology of Early Bible History," in *The Seventh-day Day Adventist Bible Commentary* (Washington, D.C.: Review and Herald®, 1953), 1: 174–196. For the date of the Exodus as ca. 1450 B.C., see esp. W. Shea, "Exodus, Date of," *International Standard Bible Encyclopedia,* vol. 2, rev. ed. (Grand Rapids, Mich.: Eerdmans, 1982), 230–238.

10.   For additional evidence, including the thirty universal expressions describing the Genesis Flood, see R. M. Davidson, "Biblical Evidence for the Universality of the Genesis Flood," *Origins* 22, no. 2 (1995): 58–73; and Davidson, "The Genesis Flood Narrative: Crucial Issues in the Current Debate," *Andrews University Seminary Studies* 42, no. 1 (2004): 49–77. Beyond the evidence cited in the main text of this book, I summarize thirteen additional lines of biblical evidence supporting the global nature of the Flood: (1) the genealogical lines from both Adam (Gen. 4:17–26; 5:1–31) and Noah (Gen. 10:1–32; 11:1–9) are exclusive in nature, indicating that as Adam was father of all pre-Flood humanity, so Noah was father of all post-Flood humanity, thus clearly implying that all humanity on the globe outside of the ark perished in the Flood; (2) the same inclusive divine blessing "Be fruitful and multiply" is given to both Adam and Noah (Gen. 1:28; 9:1), indicating that Noah is a "new Adam," repopulating the world as did the first Adam; (3) the New Testament passages concerning the Flood all employ universal language (e.g., "swept

them *all* away" [Matt. 24:39, CEV; emphasis added]; "destroyed them *all*" [Luke 17:27, NIV; emphasis added]; "he did not spare the ancient *world*, . . . when he brought a flood upon the *world* of the ungodly" [2 Pet. 2:5; emphasis added]; Noah "condemned the *world*" [Heb. 11:7; emphasis added]); and (4) the New Testament Flood typology assumes and *depends upon* the global extent of the Flood; just as there was a global flood in the time of Noah, so there will be a global judgment by fire at the end of time (2 Pet. 3:6, 7).

The next lines of biblical evidence for a global flood point to some of the numerous universal terms or expressions in Gen. 6–9 indicating the global scope of the Flood; (5) "the earth" (Gen. 6:12, 13, 17), without any limiting descriptor, harks back to the same expression in the global creation (Gen. 1:1, 2, 10); (6) "the face of all the earth" (Gen. 7:3; cf. 8:9) echoes the same phrase in the global context of creation (Gen. 1:29); (7) "face of the ground" (Gen. 7:4, 22, 23; 8:8), in parallel with "face of the whole earth" (Gen. 8:9), links with its usage in the context of global creation (Gen. 2:6); (8) "all flesh" (thirteen times in Gen. 6–9) is accompanied by additional phrases that recall the global creation of animals and man (Gen. 1:24, 30; 2:7); (9) "every living thing of all flesh" (Gen. 6:19; cf. 9:16), and the similar expression "all living things that I have made" (Gen. 7:4, NKJV), the latter specifically referring back to creation; (10) "all existence [*kol hayqum*]" (Gen. 7:4, 23, footnote) is one of the most inclusive terms available to the Hebrew writer to express totality of life; (11) "all that was on the dry land" (Gen. 7:22, NKJV) indicates the global extent of the Flood and clarifies that this worldwide destruction is limited to terrestrial creatures; (12) "under the whole heaven" (Gen. 7:19, NKJV), a phrase always universal elsewhere in Scripture (see, e.g., Exod. 17:14; Deut. 4:19); and (13) "all the fountains of the great deep [*tehom*]" (Gen. 7:11, NKJV; cf. 8:2) harks back to the same expression in Gen. 1:2. The many links with the global creation in Gen. 1 and 2 show that the Flood is an eschatological, step-by-step global "uncreation" followed by a step-by-step global "re-creation."

11. J. Barr, letter to D. C. C. Watson, April 23, 1984. Barr continues, "Or, to put it negatively, the apologetic arguments which suppose the 'days' of creation to be long eras of time, the figures of years not to be chronological, and the flood to be a merely local Mesopotamian flood, are not taken seriously by any such professors, as far as I know." (However, Barr, as a critical scholar, would no doubt go on to say that science has shown us that the writers of Genesis were wrong about these historical matters.) An update of Barr's statement is in J. Davis, "24 Hours—Plain As Day," *Answers* 7 (Apr.-June 2012): 66–69, http://www.answersingenesis.org/articles/am/v7/n2/24-hours. Those who move in a different direction from this interpretation are mainly evangelical scholars who are seeking to find a way to harmonize Scripture with what they consider to be the "assured results" of science. See, e.g., K. W. Giberson and F. S. Collins, *The Language of Science and Faith: Straight Answers to Genuine Questions* (Downers Grove, Ill.: InterVarsity, 2011), 69–70; and R. F. Carlson and T. Longman III, *Science, Creation and the Bible: Reconciling Rival Theories*

of Origins (Downers Grove, Ill.: InterVarsity Press, 2010), 13.

12. The Bible was prepared for our instruction, but there was a deeper purpose. If Jesus was to accomplish His mission of redeeming lost humanity, He could not have any advantage over us. Consequently, while He was on earth, He didn't have the divine knowledge He had in heaven, and the Holy Spirit couldn't communicate with Him in any way that we don't have access to. How could He as an innocent child and adult escape Satan's vicious deceptions? As we would expect, He planned ahead. He gave Himself a very great advantage, and we have access to the same advantage if we will accept it. He inspired His servants to write the book that He knew He would read in His earthly life—the Old Testament. This book had to be factual and accurate. It revealed to Jesus who He was, who Satan is, and the history of the conflict between Himself and Satan. From the Old Testament, Jesus learned about the literal Creation week and the Sabbath and what this tells us about our relationship to our Creator.

A few years ago, one of us (Davidson) summarized some of this evidence in a paper read at an annual meeting of the Evangelical Theological Society (which is attended by evangelical scholars from many countries). After the presentation, a revered, Harvard-trained Old Testament scholar, arguably the dean of Old Testament scholars until his recent death, came up to me and remarked privately: "You Seventh-day Adventists are virtually the only denomination that still unabashedly and officially affirms the biblical truths concerning earth's origins. Please, do not give up your strong stand for a literal seven-day Creation week and a global flood."

CHAPTER 5

THE BIBLE CONTRIBUTES SCIENTIFIC INSIGHTS

In some cases, we have described how our growing scientific understanding improved our interpretation of the Bible, such as with cosmology and the fixity of species. Now we will turn to other situations in which the conflict (stage 1) was resolved or is being resolved (stages 2 and 3) by the reverse—confidence in the truth of the Bible inspired scientists to further research, which then resulted in better insights (stage 3).

In this type of research we don't attempt to find scientific explanations for supernatural events, as some critics have claimed. Science can never study miracles or show us whether they could occur. However, miracles can have discernible effects on the earth and on its history. For example, if God caused a flood that tore up the surface of the whole earth and then in a relatively short time laid down all the sediments it was carrying, that extremely widespread and deeply catastrophic flood must have left evidence—physical remains—that point to its reality. We, then, can investigate the evidence such an event must have left behind, especially since Scripture says it happened relatively recently.

Forests, fossils, and dead whales

In the 1960s and early 1970s, the multiple layers of fossil forests in Yellowstone National Park were commonly portrayed as exhibit A of the evidence contradicting the Bible's depiction of life as having existed on earth only a relatively short time. Scientists claimed each of those fossil forests would have taken a very long time to form, and there were many layers of fossils. In fact, it was believed that the layers of fossil forests established the existence of a cycle: Over a period of up to one thousand years, the trees in an area would grow up and become a mature forest. But then that forest would be killed, buried, and fossilized as a result of volcanic eruptions. Eventually, another forest would grow on top of the fossilized forest. Then there'd be another volcanic eruption, followed again by the growth of another forest, and so forth. The scientists who studied the site had concluded that this lengthy cycle had been repeated more than a hundred times.

However, research done by creationist scientists found evidence that the forests didn't grow one after the other.[1] Instead, it is more likely that repeated volcanic mudflows transported and buried uprooted dead trees in the upright positions in which they were found—which had actually occurred when Mount Saint Helens erupted in 1980. This new interpretation of the evidence didn't require the many lengthy cycles of the former theory. It could have happened in a relatively short time.

Here's another case: The Coconino Sandstone in northern Arizona is interpreted as being an accumulation of ancient desert sand dunes that over time have become sandstone. The only fossils in the Coconino Sandstone are fossil animal tracks. Some have argued that these tracks are evidence that the Coconino sand deposits are the remains of an ancient desert. However, some Christian scientists wanted to understand how the Coconino Sandstone fit into Noah's Flood, so they studied the evidence. They found that the evidence unequivocally indicates that the tracks had to have been made *entirely underwater.*[2] Furthermore, the evidence requires more water than mere ponds in the desert would supply; to have underwater "dunes," one must have a significant amount of water.

The Coconino Sandstone deposit offers other evidence of a recent, extensive flood. This deposit rests on top of the red mudstone of the Hermit Shale layer. There are cracks in the top of the Hermit Shale, some of which are up to twenty-five feet (eight meters) deep, and they're filled with the white Coconino Sandstone. Geological literature describes these as mud cracks, or "desiccation cracks," and says they were caused when the red aquatic mud deposit that had been there dried up when the climate changed and the area became a desert. Then the Coconino sand filled the cracks in the Hermit Shale layer, and eventually both formations became rock.

This scenario is marred by a number of problems, but conventional geologic theory didn't stimulate anyone to question it. However, research motivated by the biblical worldview has demonstrated that the cracks aren't the product of desiccation. Instead, the Hermit Shale was covered by the Coconino layer, and some time later this sand, still uncemented, was injected into the red mud below, apparently because of pressure produced by earthquakes.[3]

These two studies indicate the Coconino Sandstone didn't originate as desert dunes. The sand didn't slowly cover the mud flat after the mud had dried and cracked in the sun. Instead, the mud and sand were deposited under water, and when the mud and the overlying sand were still soft, the sand was forced down into the mud. This could all have happened rapidly and is not like the normal geological forces we see today.

One more example: in Peru, the Miocene-Pliocene Pisco Formation contains many thousands of fossil whales that were buried in thick sediments composed of sand and the skeletons of microscopic diatoms. Previous study by geologists and paleontologists interpreted the sediment as having accumulated slowly, only a few centimeters of it being added each thousand years.

Then a group of Bible-oriented creationists began to study this whale cemetery. They soon noticed something that hadn't caught the attention of previous researchers: the whales and other fossil vertebrates are exquisitely preserved. That isn't possible unless the animals were buried rapidly soon after they died—within weeks or months for each individual animal, rather than thousands of years.[4] And at the rate of a few inches of precipitate every thousand years, it would have taken four thousand years to cover something just ten inches in diameter—hardly fast enough to preserve organic material "exquisitely"!

We could add a number of other examples; but the ones we have described are enough to demonstrate that a biblical worldview can open our eyes to scientific insights that others could have found, but didn't. In *every case* in which scientists have taken this approach while using careful scientific methodology, they have made progress toward resolving what seem to be conflicts between scientific "facts" and the Bible. We argue that confidence in the Bible combined with careful scientific research procedures can result in scientific advances, not in spite of but *because of* trust in the Bible's account of origins and the history of life on earth.[5] There are, we suggest, vast opportunities for more of this type of research.

On the other hand, geological and paleontological research has found other phenomena that seem incompatible with a Bible-based belief in short-age geology (the theory that there have been only a few thousand years between the creation of life and the present). These phenomena seem to indicate that life must have existed on earth much longer than short-age geology claims. Thus, these are issues that are in stage 1 conflict.

What should we conclude from these challenges? We face at least two possibilities. We can conclude that the Bible is wrong and that the earth has existed for millions of years, during which time evolution has shaped life on the earth. Or we can take the position that scientific discoveries yet to be made will call for a reinterpretation of these lines of evidence.

As we have seen, that has already been the case for some phenomena we've discussed. When scientists haven't settled for answers that contradict the Bible's picture of earth history, but have instead continued to study the evidence, they *have* been able to resolve the conflicts.

Do we have reason to hope for more of this type of progress, or have we reached the end of the line for stage 3 solutions? We will address these important questions in what follows in this book.

ENDNOTES

1. H. G. Coffin, "Orientation of Trees in the Yellowstone Petrified Forests," *Journal of Paleontology* 50 (1976): 539–543; Coffin, "The Organic Levels of the Yellowstone Petrified Forests," *Origins* 6, no. 2 (1979): 71–82; Coffin, "Erect Floating Stumps in Spirit Lake, Washington," *Geology* 11 (1983): 298, 299; Coffin, "Erect Floating Stumps in Spirit Lake, Washington: Reply," *Geology* 11 (1983): 734; A. V. Chadwick, and T. Yamamoto, "A Paleoecological Analysis of the Petrified Trees in the Specimen Creek Area of Yellowstone National Park, Montana, USA," *Palaeogeography, Palaeoclimatology, Palaeoecology* 45 (1984): 39–48.

2. L. Brand, "Field and Laboratory Studies on the Coconino

Sandstone (Permian) Vertebrate Footprints and Their Paleoecological Implications," *Palaeogeography, Palaeoclimatology, Palaeoecology* 28 (1979): 25–38; (reprinted in W. A. S. Sarjeant, ed., "Terrestrial Trace Fossils," *Benchmark Papers in Geology* 76 [1983]: 126–139); L. Brand and T. Tang, "Fossil Vertebrate Footprints in the Coconino Sandstone (Permian) of Northern Arizona: Evidence for Underwater Origin," *Geology* 19 (1991): 1201–1204; L. Brand, "Reply: Fossil Vertebrate Footprints in the Coconino Sandstone (Permian) of Northern Arizona: Evidence for Underwater Origin," *Geology* 20 (1992): 668–670; L. Brand, "Variations in Salamander Trackways Resulting From Substrate Differences," *Journal of Paleontology* 70 (1996): 1004–1010.

3. J. H. Whitmore and R. Strom, "Sand Injectites at the Base of the Coconino Sandstone, Grand Canyon, Arizona (USA)," *Sedimentary Geology* 230 (2010): 46–59.

4. R. L. Esperante-Caamano, L. R. Brand, A. Chadwick, and O. Poma, "Taphonomy of Fossil Whales in the Diatomaceous Sediments of the Miocene/Pliocene Pisco Formation, Peru," in *Current Topics on Taphonomy and Fossilization,* eds. M. De Renzi, M. Alonso, M. Belinchon, E. Penalver, P. Montoya, and A. Marquez-Aliaga, (Valencia, Spain: Ayuntamiento de Valencia, 2002), 337–343; L. Brand, R. Esperante, A. Chadwick, O. Poma, and M. Alomia, "Fossil Whale Preservation Implies High Diatom Accumulation Rate in the Miocene-Pliocene Pisco Formation of Peru," *Geology* 32 (2004): 165–168.

5. L. Brand, "How Do We Know What Is True?" *Journal of Adventist Education* 73, no. 2 (Dec. 2010/Jan. 2011): 16–23.

Chapter 6

STAGE 1 CONFLICTS AND THE ORIGIN OF EVIL

No doubt radiometric dating belongs at the top of our list of stage 1 phenomena. Creationists have done some interesting work on this issue, but much of the theory and of the body of evidence is still in direct conflict with a timescale that says life-forms have lived on earth for only a few thousand years. How should we relate to this problem?

To find the answer, we will first of all need to deal with a very foundational question: *Because science gave us a better understanding of the Bible regarding the theories of geocentricity and of the fixity of species, why not allow radiometric dates to show us that the Bible was wrong when it didn't allow for millions of years of geological time? Why take a different approach with radiometric dating?*

This isn't a trivial question. It involves a crucial choice.

There is a significant difference between the implications of the fixity of species and the implications of conventional geological time. The nature of this difference is critical for all Christians because it addresses the very foundations of Christianity—the reliability of Scripture and the gospel, and the character of God. Nothing in the Bible conflicts with the theory that species can change, but the implications of geological time differ greatly from Scripture.

The great controversy and the salvation story hold together only if human sin is responsible for the moral evil (human greed, theft, murder, etc.) and natural evil (suffering and death from volcanoes, storms, and earthquakes, etc.) on the earth, as Scripture declares. If God chose to create life through the workings of evolution over millions of years, then moral and natural evil aren't intruders; they're integral parts of God's creation process. Furthermore, if creation were by evolution, then human sin couldn't be responsible for the presence of evil on this earth because humans are found only in the upper (last) part of the fossil record, while suffering and death extend all the way back to earth's beginning.

Efforts to contrive a way out of this logic have not been successful. Is it possible to reconcile the biblical Creation account with eons of evolution, and yet not blame God for the existence of evil? The issues we're raising demand better answers than we have. However, we do have some helpful background material. We'll take a look at it now.

Fossils, the origin of evil, and the foundation of Christianity

Why do conservative Christians object to the suggestion

that the earth has experienced millions of years of evolution? In the first place, we do so because we see reasons to believe that the history of humankind that God has revealed to us in the Bible is factual and trustworthy. And second, the origin and existence of evil have implications for the character of God. Is He responsible for evil and the suffering it brings us? If He created this earth, how can He be innocent of the evil that is spread across its face? The answers to these questions have both biblical and scientific aspects. The Bible's account of Creation reveals that God is innocent. But what do the fossils and the history of humans and of suffering say? We will now examine the perspective of science. We'll start with fossils.

There's an oddity about the distribution of human fossils in the fossil record. They're only in the uppermost part—in other words, the most recent part—of the fossil record.

Why?

The connection between rocks and fossils and a biblical understanding of evil is very important but not immediately obvious. A backyard analogy will serve to introduce the link.

It isn't unusual for us to see flowing water deposit layers of mud or sand in a streambed or maybe even in our backyard. If our backyard were to be flooded five times before we could clean it up, we'd have a muddy history book to study. Obviously, the bottom layer of mud was the first one deposited, the top layer was the last to arrive, and the layers in between arrived in order from the bottom to the top. Water doesn't normally slide one mud layer between other layers that were already in place.

The geological column with its fossils works the same

way, but on a much larger scale. It contains many more layers of fossils embedded in sediment, and the bottom layer was formed first and the top layer came last.

Now our curiosity motivates us to take another step or two. We begin digging in the layers, one layer at a time, just like a paleontologist or an archaeologist. Our digging unearths some intriguing objects in the mud—particularly in the top and bottom layers—that suggest a little story about the history of our neighborhood.

In the topmost layer, we find bits of doggy poop. A few dogs do live in this neighborhood, so we use deoxyribonucleic acid (DNA) fingerprinting to trace these artifacts. This leads us to Lassie, a dog that lives nearby—in fact, just three houses down the street. We find a variety of other "treasures" in the next three layers, but no more doggy poop. And when we get to the lowest layer, we find there an abundance of apricot pits, which is surprising because we hadn't seen any in the layers above.

Now we have the material we need to construct a little biological history of the neighborhood. The evidence points to the presence of apricot trees only up to the first flood, but not after it. We can also hypothesize that Lassie didn't arrive here until the time of the last flood. The evidence seems quite clear on these points.

However, in contrast to those who are doing research on real fossils, we have the advantage of having lived throughout the time the floods took place. Thus, we have the information we need to verify or to disprove our biological hypotheses about the apricots and Lassie.

There was indeed an apricot tree in the area, and as we suspected, it was uprooted during the first flood. So far, so good. But we know that our neighbor Joe acquired Lassie some time *before the first flood*! What went wrong with our second hypothesis? How could the evidence mislead us so badly? Thoughtful reflection doesn't reveal any errors in our research procedures, so we must do more digging to resolve this dilemma.

The new shovel work arouses the neighbors' suspicions, but it reveals a critical part of the story. The fifth flood followed a slightly different path than the first four; it was the only flood that went through Lassie's yard. Lassie was there all the time, but only the last flood met the conditions that could produce evidence of his presence.

This little story is relevant to our questions about the origin of evil. Our five floods and the biological evidence connected to them are a small representation of the fossil record. There are significant principles in our little model that apply to the geological column scientists have developed. The geological column, with its fossil record, is like a history book made up of layer after layer of rock. Each of these layers contains fossils of the animals that lived when that layer was being formed.

In principle, this seems as if it would be an accurate record of what plants and animals were living on the earth during each successive period in the history of our earth. Indeed, it isn't realistic to disregard the fossil record, because it contains much valuable information for anyone seeking to understand earth's history. But we should also be wise enough to recognize some inherent uncertainties that will determine how we interpret any history written in the rocks.

FOSSIL RECORDS

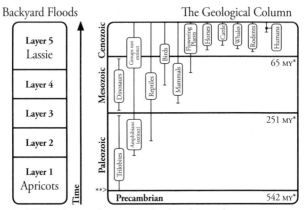

Backyard Floods · The Geological Column

* Millions of years in the conventional geological time scale.
** Beginning of the global flood catastrophe.

One documented example from real life is similar to our story of Lassie. In 1938, commercial fishermen, working the deep ocean, caught a coelacanth.[1] Fossils of this species of fish are found in early portions of the geological column, but not in the upper layers, the Cenozoic. So this fish was thought to have gone extinct sixty-five million years ago. Despite its absence from the upper portion of the fossil record, then, it must have been alive for all those presumed sixty-five million years. Evidently, the members of this species weren't living where they would be preserved in fossil form when they died—just as the circumstances of four of our neighborhood floods weren't what was needed to preserve evidence of Lassie's existence during the time they covered.

Could there be other, similar inadequacies in the fossil record because of comparable circumstances?

There could be, and this is where we come back to the origin of evil. If the presence of evil on this earth was the result of Adam and Eve's sin, then they must have sinned at or near the beginning of the fossil record, because that record is full of earthquakes, floods, and volcanoes; and disease, death, and extinction. But if the original pair sinned low on the geological column—in other words, near the beginning of the fossil record—then why are human fossils found only in the uppermost portion of the fossil record at the *end* of the fossil record instead of at its beginning? If humans didn't exist until the final episode in the fossil record of animal history began to play, then how could their sin open the door to disease, death, and all the other destruction recorded in the rocks all through the geological column?

Another hypothesis

We can propose a geological hypothesis to explain this mismatch between fossil history and the fall of Adam and Eve that brought evil into the world. Our hypothesis proposes that during much of the fossil record humans and some common modern plants and animals were living, but not where fossils were forming.[2] Could humans and the extinct

Cambrian animals all have been living on earth for millions of years without leaving any fossil evidence of their existence? It is extremely unlikely that all humans would have escaped becoming fossilized during such a long time. But in the biblical scenario, the fossils are a record of death during a global flood and its aftermath, and, perhaps, even between the Fall and the Flood. We have never seen a global flood, so we don't know exactly how this would have all worked, but such a rapid sequence of events offers more plausible possibilities for keeping some groups of animals out of the early part of the fossil record.

If that hypothesis is true, it would allow Adam and Eve's fall to occur at the *beginning* of the fossil record and thus explain the entrance of evil on planet Earth before fossils formed. The story of a literal, seven-day Creation week, with Adam and Eve in the Garden of Eden, where they succumb to the tempter and invite evil into their world, was at the *beginning*. Then, after sin and evil entered the picture, the fossil record—formed during and after the Flood catastrophe—documented further evidence of the evil, pain, and death that have become a part of earth's story.

So, the available evidence doesn't rule out the hypothesis that humans were contemporary with Cambrian life-forms but weren't living where fossils were forming. That's helpful, but can we go further and find evidence to support it? In our backyard flood story, human memory held the information necessary to test our hypotheses. And the hypothesis about the extinction of the coelacanths was disproved by catching live ones. Do we have access to evidence that can provide that level of confidence about the origin of evil? Where can we find a record of just when humans first appeared on earth?

Unless we find human fossils near the bottom of the fossil record (comparable in significance to catching a live coelacanth), our hypothesis about the lack of human fossils could be tested only by written history, and that from someone who was present all through fossil history. The Bible is the only publication that claims to have such a record. With most scientists, this source carries no weight, so it all comes down to our answer to this question: do we have more confidence in the biblical record or in modern human interpretations of the fossil record?

Interpretations

Of course the hypothesis that humans existed on earth at the time that the Cambrian record was being laid down also has other implications. It challenges, among other things, current interpretations of radiometric evidence and the conventional geological timescale with its millions of years. You can see in the figure above that mammals, birds, flowering plants (including fruit trees), and living groups of amphibians are found only in the upper half of the fossil record. The most familiar types of mammals, such as cattle, horses, dogs, whales, and rodents, are limited to an even higher part of the fossil record.[3] These organisms—and human beings—either were living at the time of the Cambrian fossils but weren't being buried and fossilized during that time, or else cattle, horses, fruit trees, and the other familiar life-forms didn't evolve until long after the initial creation event.

Will the Lassie explanation work for them as well as for humans? There is reason to think that animals living in upland habitats usually didn't get fossilized. Did humans and trilobites live on earth at the same time, but in different places or in different habitats? The Bible record implies that this must have been essentially the situation; but because we weren't there, we are left with intriguing questions about details.

These and other lines of evidence are big issues, but ultimately the choice we make must be based on who we believe knows more about earth history—finite humans, who didn't see the forming of fossils, or the infinite God, who did—and who inspired the writers of the Bible. In whom do we place our trust?

ENDNOTES

1. M. J. Benton, *Vertebrate Palaeontology,* 3rd ed. (Malden, Mass.: Blackwell Publishing, 2005), 70.

2. Brand, *Faith, Reason, and Earth History,* 397, 398.

3. Benton, *Vertebrate Palaeontology,* 329–362.

Chapter 7

The Rise of
Theistic Evolution

Charles Darwin was greatly bothered by the evil in nature. He couldn't believe a good God created despicable predators and parasites; his theory attributed their existence to the impersonal forces of evolution.[1] But Darwin apparently wasn't concerned about reconciling his theory with the Bible.

In the century and a half since Darwin's day, many Christian scholars have struggled to make such a reconciliation. Darwinism has won their allegiance, and many of them have sought ways to blend Christianity with the rise of life-forms through eons of evolution. Some envision God as visiting earth periodically as the millions of years rolled on, and at each visit creating some new groups of animals and plants, leaving each group to evolve as time continues. This approach is called "progressive creation."

A more common compromise is known as theistic evolution.

All the versions of this concept picture life originating from nonliving materials and, over hundreds of millions of years, evolving into all the life-forms that have lived on earth, including the evolution of humans from other primates. Those who hold this view credit God with being involved in the process in some indirect way; thus, it is called "theistic evolution," or "evolutionary creation."[2]

Because theistic evolutionists seek harmony with mainline science, they minimize God's involvement in evolution, restricting it to subtle roles that science can't detect. They seem to believe that if they keep God confined in a narrow enough space, there is no need to worry that science will disprove His existence or His activity in the universe.

Many theistic evolutionists argue that God could grant the universe and the human race freedom only by evolving life—allowing life to "make itself" through the process of "chance and necessity"—mutation and natural selection. They also point to quantum uncertainty, the unpredictability that is a characteristic of the particles within atoms, as perhaps being the place within the universe where freedom comes to life.[3]

However, in all we have read, we have never found an explanation of how quantum uncertainty at the subatomic level can create the organization and operation of neural networks in the human brain that result in free will. The claim that our free will, the freedom to choose that is ours, is evidence supporting only the theory of evolution implies that God doesn't know how to design a brain that can exercise freedom of choice. Theistic evolution is a philosophy that discards Genesis as a source of truth about history and replaces it with the theory of evolution. God is, for the most part, on the sidelines, where He can't interfere with our chosen theories.

Theistic evolution and evil

To evaluate the possibility of reconciling theistic evolution with the Bible, we need to know how believers in theistic evolution explain the origin of evil. Can the character of God, the reality of an evil world, and theistic evolution be tied into a coherent package? The God described in the Bible is a loving God who shed tears over His chosen nation, the Israelites, when they refused to accept His offer of blessings and salvation. He also is all knowing, all wise, and all powerful—capable of instantly replacing crippled muscles with new living tissue, and even of raising the dead—as Jesus demonstrated repeatedly in His healings. But if evolution were God's chosen method of creating, then we must give up at least one of those characteristics of God.

The explanations of why evil exists given by theistic evolutionists fall into three categories:[4]

1. God isn't good. He doesn't care about the suffering and death of His creatures.
2. God isn't all powerful. Creation by means of evolution was the best that He could do.
3. God isn't all knowing. He can't foresee the future, so He didn't know how much suffering and death evolution would cause. And if He didn't realize

the effects evolution would have, then we can't blame Him for them.

To summarize those three explanations more bluntly: either God is cruel or He isn't all powerful or He isn't very smart.[5] Those might be suitable descriptions of the ancient pagan gods, but they are all tragic caricatures of the God of the Bible.

Some individuals still seek to combine somehow the ideas that there is a Creator God, that humans and other life-forms arose by evolution, that God didn't originate evil, and that the Bible is an inspired document that is reliable and worthy of our trust. However, this approach is problematic; it seeks to harmonize inherently contradictory concepts.

The biblical story of the great controversy explains the origin of evil in simple, believable terms: God creates a perfect universe in which there is no evil. Morally free created beings rebel, introducing evil, pain, and death. And then God Himself endures pain as He provides the sacrifice of His Son to redeem us from all the aspects of evil that sin produces. Any other explanation makes God the author of evil.

If the biblical story of a literal creation by a loving God followed by sin and evil is correct, why are so many scientists uncompromisingly opposed to it? The answer has as much to do with philosophy as with science.

Endnotes

1. C. G. Hunter, *Darwin's God: Evolution and the Problem of Evil*

(Grand Rapids, Mich.: Brazos Press, 2001); Hunter, *Science's Blind Spot* (Grand Rapids, Mich.: Brazos Press, 2007).

2. A. Peacocke, *Theology for a Scientific Age* (Minneapolis: Fortress Press, 1993); J. Polkinghorne, *Science and Theology* (Minneapolis: Fortress Press, 1998); I. G. Barbour, *When Science Meets Religion* (New York: Harper Collins, 2000); N. Murphey, *Religion and Science* (Kitchener, Ontario: Pandora Press, 2002); D. O. Lamoureux, *Evolutionary Creation* (Eugene, Ore.: Wipf & Stock, 2008); F. S. Collins, *The Language of God* (New York: Free Press, 2006); L. Brand, "A Biblical Perspective on the Philosophy of Science," *Origins* 59 (2006): 6–42, http://www.grisda.org /origins/59006.pdf.

Theistic evolution is embraced by proponents of so-called temple theology. According to a popular version of this theology, God allowed life to evolve for millions of years, and then there was a week of celebration of the finished "creation"— the Creation week of Gen. 1 and 2. See, e.g., J. H. Walton, *The Lost World of Genesis One: Ancient Cosmology and the Origins Debate* (Downers Grove, Ill.: InterVarsity, 2009).

3. Peacocke, *Theology for a Scientific Age,* 99–127, 152–160; J. Polkinghorne, *Quarks, Chaos and Christianity* (New York: Crossroad Publishing, 1994), 36–50; Polkinghorne, *Science and Theology,* 76–81; Brand, "Philosophy of Science," 6–42.

4. R. Rice, "Creation, Evolution, and Evil," in *Understanding Genesis,* eds. B. Bull, F. Guy, and E. Taylor (Riverside, Calif.: Adventist Today Foundation, 2006), 10–22. A common fourth category is to ignore the problem and simply insist repeatedly that there is no conflict between evolution and the Bible—without giving

any supporting evidence, textual analysis, or other explanation.

5. E. E. Zinke, "Theistic Evolution: Implications for the Role of Creation in Seventh-day Adventist Theology," in *Creation, Catastrophe and Calvary,* ed. J. T. Baldwin (Hagerstown, Md.: Review and Herald®, 2000), 159–171.

CHAPTER 8

SCIENCE AND NATURALISM

In this, the second decade of the twenty-first century A.D., the conventional scientific community maintains a commitment to a millions-of-years evolutionary scenario, and they maintain it with more unified passion than ever before. More surprisingly, almost the entire community of Christian scholars has accepted the same scenario in the form of theistic evolution. We can't just wave that off, can we? Doesn't all this support for the theory of evolution from those who should be in the know suggest that the evidence is compelling? Or is there some other explanation for the unity of belief in millions of years of evolution and evil?

There *is* another explanation. To find it, we will very briefly review several hundred years of history. Wars are best understood in light of what preceded them. Science also has a history that will help us find the explanation we seek.

When a road is slippery and one is sliding toward the ditch, it's easy to overcorrect and end up in the ditch on the other side of the road. Similarly, when solving problems, humans sometimes go too far and end up creating the opposite problem.

Before science entered the modern era during which it has been highly successful, those who were interested in how the world operates considered the ancient Greek masters as the authorities for their discipline. Only gradually did they escape this ditch as they learned to correct their old ideas and to expect to make their scientific discoveries by looking toward the future rather than toward the past. At the same time, the desire to escape all sources of authority—including dogmatic, authoritarian religion and the equally authoritarian, despotic governments in the Middle Ages—was growing.[1]

At this time, scientists were abandoning another mistaken practice. For centuries, they had been prone to give mystical explanations for the things they didn't understand.[2] But the research they did slowly taught them that God normally manages the universe through the consistent, understandable laws that He created. For example, through research, William Harvey (1578–1657) learned that blood doesn't circulate throughout the body because mystical spiritual forces make it flow, but because the heart is a pump, a mechanism that can be understood. For science to reach its potential, scientists had to learn to avoid depending on ancient authority and on facile, mystical explanations.

However, in escaping that ditch, scientists inexorably began to slide across the road toward the other ditch—toward the tyranny of another kind of authoritarianism. As they moved away from dependence on authorities such as the ancient

Greeks, they also left behind their confidence in the Bible. They moved instead into strict naturalism—the assumption that there have *never* been any miracles, and that no god or other intelligent agent ever had a part in the origin of the universe or of living organisms. They slid across the road into believing that everything that exists came into being through the normal, unaided operation of the laws of chemistry and physics.[3] Nothing else was involved.

Scientists can't study miracles the way they study natural events—even creationists can understand that. How could we determine what process Jesus used to turn water into wine? Nor can science provide us with a way to determine whether or not He really *did* turn water to wine. That's beyond the reach of science. In these matters, about all we can do is to humbly recognize that we don't know what God can or cannot do.

To make our way through these issues, we must maintain a thoughtful balance. When we explore nature in a chemistry laboratory, scientific success depends on our not assuming that God might tinker with the chemicals in our experiment. We must trust that careful research will reveal the laws that govern chemical reactions. Scientific research has taught us that God doesn't normally tinker with the universe. He normally uses His incredibly beautiful and effective laws of chemistry and physics to make it work. But if God's Word tells us that He has performed miracles in the past and He still performs them today—especially in creation and in His reaching out to people who need His help—does it help science find truth if it arbitrarily says that He couldn't in the past and doesn't do so today? If we declare that no one ever has the power or the authority to do miracles, we're making that up. Is God going to feel bound not to cross a line *that we've made up*?

In the case of the Flood, the possibility that one or more miracles were involved is consistent with the power of the God we worship. Surely a global flood on the scale that Scripture portrays would be a huge geological event—one that must have left some evidence on earth's surface so that the methods and tools of science would enable us to detect it.

Instead of searching with open minds to learn from the evidence around us, many scientists have adopted the philosophical assumption that science must never accept the possibility of an intelligent, all-powerful God who performs miracles such as creating life and influencing geological events. Many subscribe to a form of this philosophy called "methodological naturalism." They accept the possible existence of God, but only if He doesn't do anything that we could notice—certainly no miracles.[4]

This virus of naturalism dominates scientific thinking today, especially in the study of origins—of biological and geological history. When one is using experiments to study the ongoing processes of chemistry, physics, and biology, it isn't appropriate to suggest that God is miraculously altering our experiments. However, studying history and origins is a different matter. In that study, miracles can't be ruled out. We maintain that while science has escaped from the ditch of belief in a god who tinkers with the universe on a daily basis, it has fallen into the ditch on the other side of the road—the dogmatic assumption of naturalism.

This assumption (including the application of methodological naturalism to origins) doesn't allow any explanation that implies supernatural action at any time in the history of the universe. Take, for instance, the naturalistic hypothesis that the original life-forms arose by themselves and not as the result of actions taken by a supernatural, intelligent being. Even if every scientific attempt to find support for that hypothesis fails (which they have so far), naturalism dictates that science must still confidently declare that life arose with no intelligent input, *no matter the evidence*. Why? Because the naturalistic assumption demands it; apart from abandoning naturalism, there is no appeal from this demand.

Generations of scientists have been educated to accept naturalism and to use it to guide their scholarly thinking, to inspire their hypotheses, and to govern their interpretations of research. All data must be interpreted in light of naturalism's assumptions. The previous few sentences may seem too strong, but they are abundantly supported in the writings of scientists and of theologians who follow their lead.[5] If we challenge the assumption of naturalism, those writers will say, "You're the one who doesn't understand. Science can't accept miracles." We have heard and read this sentiment many times from prominent scientists and philosophers. There is reason to think that many scientists don't really accept this rigid form of naturalism, but they don't know how to challenge it or they consider it too risky to try.

Theologians who are theistic evolutionists base their

theology on the foundation of belief that evolution has been at work from the earth's beginning. They appear, it seems, to be unaware that the unity of the commitment of those in the sciences to evolution and deep time (the billions of years scientists believe the earth has existed more or less in its current form) is rooted in naturalism, which denies the possibility of the Bible being correct about these issues. It seems to be unwise, circular reasoning to use an assumption invented by humans claiming that there never were any miracles, to determine whether there is a miracle-working God. This point is at the core of the big issues we are discussing. Those who rush to be compatible with the majority of the scholarly world often don't recognize the circular reasoning that they are accepting.

Science's rejection of supernatural creation is based partly on its interpretation of the evidence. But the primary reason for that rejection is the assumption that only naturalism has a true picture of the processes and laws that have governed the origin of our world and the events it has experienced throughout history.

Even though we disagree with this approach, we can't ignore the evidence that science brings to the table. So, to better understand what science is saying about origins, we'll look at more of the evidence later in this book.

ENDNOTES

1. A. McGrath, *The Twilight of Atheism* (New York: Doubleday, 2004).
2. J. Gribbin, *Science: A History* (New York: Penguin Books, 2002).

3. R. Dawkins, *The Blind Watchmaker* (New York: W. W. Norton, 1986); R. Lewontin, "Billions and Billions of Demons," review of *The Demon-Haunted World: Science as a Candle in the Dark,* by C. Sagan, *New York Review of Books*, Jan. 9, 1997, 28–32; K. B. Miller, "The Misguided Attack on Methodological Naturalism," in *For the Rock Record,* eds. J. L. Schneiderman and W. D. Allmon (Berkeley, Calif.: University of California Press, 2009), 117–140; C. De Duve, "Mysteries of Life: Is There 'Something Else'?" in *The Nature of Nature: Examining the Role of Naturalism in Science,* eds. B. L. Gordon and W. A. Dembski (Wilmington, Del.: ISI Books, 2011), 346–357.

4. R. T. Pennock, *Tower of Babel* (Cambridge, Mass.: MIT Press, 1999), 191–206; Miller, "Methodological Naturalism," 117–140. Philosophical naturalism (PN) maintains there is no god. Methodological naturalism (MN) is the scientific method that doesn't use the supernatural as an explanation. That is actually an appropriate concept in the study of ongoing processes of nature—in a laboratory study of how chemical and physical processes work. But when MN is applied to origins and ancient history (and this is done routinely), it is a very different matter. In practice, both PN and MN have the same effect. They dogmatically deny supernatural explanations for anything, including origins and geological history. That is philosophy, not science, as scientists could never test the hypothesis of naturalism.

5. Dawkins, *The Blind Watchmaker*. There is another side to this. David Lack, a biologist, wrote a book on the evolution of finches on the Galapagos Islands (D. Lack, *Darwin's Finches*

[Cambridge: Cambridge University Press, 1947]). He also wrote a book on theology. An evolutionary biologist friend of ours said, "David Lack didn't know what to do with the evidence for evolution, but he was not willing to give up on God." There is reason to think there are many other scientists who, like David Lack, are also searching for answers.

CHAPTER 9

CONFLICT OF INTEREST

The sum of the whole matter at this point, we argue, is that the theory of large-scale evolution, with its millions of years of life on earth, is in direct conflict with Bible-based Christianity and the great controversy between Christ and Satan. If a literal, one-week creation is not true, then God's "creation" process included eons of evil, suffering, disease, natural disasters, and death—all beginning long before humans and human sin came on the scene.[1] And if the timescale in the Bible isn't true, then our confidence in the truth of other parts of Scripture is, logically, undermined. These are among the reasons many of us hold to the biblical timescale and reject the conclusion that an evolutionary process has produced the major types of organisms.

One can't fit together two contradictory stories. If there were no Garden of Eden and no fall of Adam and Eve into sin, we would have no reason to believe in the salvation story. If there were no literal creation by God, there would be no basis for worship;[2] the Bible clearly states that God is worthy of our worship because He is our Creator.[3]

We don't often agree with the outspoken atheist Richard Dawkins, but we do agree with him when he states, "Oh, but of course, the story of Adam and Eve was only ever *symbolic*, wasn't it? *Symbolic*? So, in order to impress himself, Jesus had himself tortured and executed, in vicarious punishment for a *symbolic* sin committed by a *non-existent* individual?"[4] "I think the evangelical Christians have really sort of got it right in a way, in seeing evolution as the enemy. Whereas the more, what shall we say, sophisticated theologians are quite happy to live with evolution, I think they're deluded. I think the evangelicals have got it right, in that there really is a deep incompatibility between evolution and Christianity."[5]

Our Bible-based attempts to develop scientific models of earth history must account for events in the biblical great controversy theme,[6] events that include (1) the sudden appearance of life-forms during the seven-day Creation week *before* sin and evil had appeared on the earth, and (2) rapid geological processes—including a global flood and its aftermath, which apparently also was catastrophic—that produced the geological record with its fossil evidence of complex life on earth, and all within a few thousand years. This is the biblical scenario that we can use to point the way to better geological hypotheses.

Naturalistic science will reject this approach. But our goal is not simply to follow the crowd; rather, it is to search for the best answers to our questions that we can find. With this background in mind, we can return to the issues that are still in stage 1 conflict.

ENDNOTES

1. Peacocke, *Theology for a Scientific Age,* 99–127, 152–160; Polkinghorne, *Science and Theology,* 63–65; Brand, "Philosophy of Science," 6–42.

2. While this may seem to be oversimplified here, it does point toward a profound interrelationship between origins and the other biblical doctrines. For further discussion of these interrelationships, see J. T. Baldwin, "Progressive Creationism and Biblical Revelation: Some Theological Implications," *Journal of the Adventist Theological Society* 11 (2000): 174–187; Zinke, "Theistic Evolution," 159–171; M. G. Hasel, "In the Beginning," *Adventist Review,* Oct. 25, 2001, 24–27; N. R. Gulley, "What Happens to Biblical Truth if the SDA Church Accepts Theistic Evolution?" *Journal of the Adventist Theological Society* 15, no. 2 (Autumn 2004): 40–58; R. W. Younker, "Consequences of Moving Away From a Recent Six-day Creation," *Journal of the Adventist Theological Society* 15, no. 2 (Autumn 2004): 59–70.

3. Rev. 4:11.

4. R. Dawkins, *The God Delusion* (Boston: Houghton Mifflin, 2006), 253; emphasis in original.

5. R. Dawkins, interview by H. Condor, Revelation TV, Feb. 2011, http://www.youtube.com/watch?v=Wfe4IUB9NTk.

6. White, *The Great Controversy.*

CHAPTER 10

BIBLE-BASED PREDICTIONS

The Bible pictures the earth as it is today and the life-forms on it as being relatively recent, but evolution says it has taken many millions of years for the earth and its creatures to become what they are today. Instead of simply concluding that the Bible is wrong, we suggest an alternative. We think scientific discoveries yet to be made will lead to a reinterpretation of the evidence that seems to contradict the Bible. Thus, the stage 1 conflicts that we face today will eventually be resolved.

For example, before accepting radiometric dating with its millions of years, let's go back to the Interface in our diagram on page 20. The process illustrated in that diagram doesn't allow science to dictate our theology or our theology to dictate our science. So, the conflict between the standard geological timescale and a straightforward reading of Scripture challenges us to reexamine the answers both science and the Bible have given, and to do so with even more care than we have used in the past. We're still in the conflict stage (stage 1) in assessing the issue of geological time, but there is reason to doubt the timescale of mainstream geology and to search for a different answer. Our faith doesn't depend on our resolving this conflict in our lifetime, but the continuing conflict does function as a God-given motivation to look for a solution.

Why do scientists spend their lives doing research? They're looking for insights and solutions to the questions and problems they see—to the anomalies that interest them. So, since Christian scientists do research for much the same reasons, they, too, are justified in seeking solutions for the problems that interest them.

We suggest that God has a timetable that spells out what scientific solutions will be helpful for humans to have and when they will be most helpful. The disciple Thomas was reminded that God blesses those who have faith, but that He also cares for those who have their doubts—who, like Thomas, need faith-strengthening evidence. The point is that God will give us more evidence when it will be good for us, just as He did for Thomas.[1]

We haven't resolved the conflict that radiometric dating poses, but we can say what we believe the outcome will be. We predict, based partly on faith (religion) and partly on evidence (science) that some time in the future someone will present evidence he or she has found that will show (science) that we are now seriously misinterpreting the radiometric data, and that consequently, it may actually be giving only the *relative* age of what's being tested, not the age in years. Scientists who take this prediction seriously will be in the best position to understand the new evidence if and when it appears (science) before Jesus returns to earth.

Some more predictions

Here are some additional predictions:

- We believe someone will find evidence that the laminations in ice cores are not annual layers.
- We believe someone will find that some types of stromatolites—domelike structures now thought to be built up laminae-after-laminae by living microorganisms—are not biological structures after all, but are produced in an entirely different process.
- We believe that someone will find features of the Coconino Sandstone that demonstrate that it was produced by something other than desert dune processes.
- We believe that some new evidence or some growth in our understanding of the fossil record will show that its layers do not reveal the evolution of major life-forms, as is now thought to be the case.
- Finally, we believe that sooner or later someone will find archaeological evidence that verifies the truth of the biblical account of the Exodus.

Rather than being problems for the Bible, the conflicts that led to these predictions—predictions based on both faith and science in the Interface—indicate where productive research (science) can be done and where new scientific insights can be found. Many more predictions like these can be made.

What if further research falsifies some of these predictions? What would the implications be?

Here are a couple of possibilities. First, it may indicate that the problem lies in our not being ready to draw correct conclusions, just as Galileo and his colleagues weren't ready to understand cosmology and the Bible correctly. (This may be true of the conflict about the stromatolites.) Second, we may not have enough evidence or we may not understand the phenomenon sufficiently to be able to arrive at a correct conclusion. Evidence that's incomplete can appear to falsify a prediction that actually is true. This is fairly common in science.

If science were able to falsify some of these predictions and to show that life arose through evolution over many millions of years, *then Christianity would be falsified.*

Christianity makes claims about history, and science can attempt to address some of these claims. Should this make us afraid to do research? We say No because we believe that God's Word is trustworthy. If we have confidence in the great controversy and in salvation history, we can make these predictions without fear or apology—just as long as we don't settle for quick answers and we maintain the Bible as our foundation.

Anomalies

We've looked at some observations that we believe call for more research because they don't appear to support Scripture.

Now let's look at some other phenomena that already are yielding evidence that's challenging conventional scientific theories of origins. In other words, these cases represent progress in the stage 2 research process and are approaching stage 3. We can predict that further research based on confidence in Scripture will continue to move them toward stage 3's resolution and insight.

There are biochemical reasons for believing large-scale Darwinian evolution—which posits the production of new types of organisms and the attaining of significant new biological information—to be impossible. Whole new types of organisms can arise only through an act of creation by an intelligent Being.[2] We predict that increasing evidence will, in time, establish this as a foundational principle in the eyes of everyone not so bound to naturalism as to be impervious to facts.

Other research in progress reveals reasons for doubting the long time spans called for by the standard geological timescale. These include many fossil assemblages, like the Peruvian fossil whales whose preservation was so exceptional as to constitute evidence that they must have been buried rapidly. There are also places where layers of rock that the geological column says represent many millions of years are missing. In other words, the layers above the missing ones in the geological column sit directly on the layers below where the missing layers should be, and there's no evidence of sedimentary deposits or of erosion taking place during the millions of years those missing layers should have been there. It's as if the layers that should have been covered and protected by the missing layers stood exposed to weathering for millions of years and nothing happened to them.[3] The layers should show much more evidence of erosion and other results of exposure than they do. The evidence is most consistent with the supposition that, at the very least, the layers above the missing ones were laid down a very short time after the layers that were "supposed to be" below the missing ones. Additional research, which is being done in more detail, is applying a similar concept to individual rock layers and is also raising doubts that these rocks were formed over the long periods many geologists believe were involved.

Objectivity and bias control

Could research motivated by faith perspectives introduce a bias into that research? Of course. Any worldview, religious or scientific, can introduce a bias. Leaving religious perspectives out of our science doesn't solve this problem.[4] Careful research combined with acute awareness of different viewpoints on the subject and with the quality control provided by publication in peer-reviewed literature can manage those potential biases. If biases remain, in time they will become evident with the insight that often comes with Spirit-led hindsight, and be in harmony with the biblical worldview.

The process of thought and discovery described here seeks to integrate faith and science in a thorough search for truth. Some individuals attempt to hold on to both the Bible and conventional scientific theories by keeping science and religion in separate compartments rather than seeking to integrate them into a cohesive view.[5] These efforts typically result in science providing the facts and religion seeking meaning from ancient myths and legends. When two sources address the same topic and give opposite answers, they can't both be true. And pretending that we can hold on to both and still be logically coherent doesn't help. Although some of what science says about the origin of the universe is correct, other things it says must not be.

We need to keep in mind how utterly futile it is for finite humans to think we can decide what God can or cannot do. He created the laws of nature, and He knows how to use them to accomplish His will. The story in Joshua 10:13 of the sun standing still is an example of this. We can't understand how this could have happened or at least have appeared to have happened. But we have no idea what options an infinite God has.

ENDNOTES

1. John 20:24–29.
2. L. P. Lester, and R. G. Bohlin, *The Natural Limits to Biological Change,* 2nd ed. (Dallas: Probe Books; Word Publishing, 1989); M. J. Behe, *Darwin's Black Box* (New York: Free Press, 1996); Behe, *The Edge of Evolution* (New York: Free Press, 2007); J. C. Sanford, *Genetic Entropy and the Mystery of the Genome,* 3rd ed. (Waterloo, N.Y.: FMS Publications, 2008); S. C. Meyer, *Signature in the Cell* (New York: HarperOne, 2009); L. Brand, "The Scope and Limits of the Evolutionary Process," in *Faculty*

Faith (Berrien Springs, Mich.: Andrews University Press, forthcoming).

3. A. A. Roth, "Those Gaps in the Sedimentary Layers," *Origins* 15 (1988): 75–92, http://www.grisda.org/origins/15075.htm.

4. Pearcey, *Total Truth*.

5. E.g., see S. J. Gould, *Rocks of Ages: Science and Religion in the Fullness of Life* (New York: Ballantine Publishing, 1999).

CHAPTER 11

CREATION AND THE FINAL CONFLICT

Prophecies in Daniel and Revelation indicate a date in history that began the time of the end. Seventh-day Adventists understand that period to have begun in 1798.

Another crucial waymark in prophetic time came just under fifty years later. According to Daniel's prophecies, the investigative judgment—an event closely tied to Jesus' second advent—began on October 22, 1844.[1] Interestingly, and no doubt significantly too, Charles Darwin wrote a summary of his theory of evolution in 1844. He didn't publish his book at that time; he wrote out the theory to establish his ownership of it should someone else devise the same theory later.

While Darwin didn't publish his book in 1844, someone else wrote a book that was published in that year—in fact, in October of that year. The book has great significance for Bible believers. The author was Robert Chambers, and the book was named *Vestiges of the Natural History of Creation*.[2] This book was an evolutionary explanation of living things. It didn't propose a specific mechanism for evolution, but it is credited as being one of the most significant precursors to Darwin's book—one that prepared the way for people's acceptance of his theory of evolution when it was finally published.

In other words, we might say that Satan began the first battles of his final war against God in 1844. That's when he introduced his grand scheme to turn the world away from allegiance to the Creator. If belief in the biblical Creation account can be destroyed, confidence in the personal, loving God of the Bible will be seriously undermined as well.

The Sabbath

In the fourth commandment, God claims that He created the heavens and the earth, the sea, and all that is in them in six days and then established the seventh-day Sabbath to be a reminder through all time of our origin at His command. The Bible also claims that God *recorded this account of our origin by writing it with His finger in stone*.[3] If what God wrote with His own hand is false, why would the rest of the Bible be of any interest? But if what He wrote is true, it provides us with a foundation on which we may build our lives, knowing that it can withstand whatever storms may come our way in the future.

The book of Revelation gives us more instructions. John pictures mighty angels flying in the heavens and calling with loud voices. The three angels in Revelation 14 describe the state of the cosmic conflict, the great controversy, and call us to worship the God "who made heaven and earth, the sea and the springs of water"[4]—a clear allusion to the fourth commandment, with a probable allusion to the global Flood as well.[5] At the height of the greatest battle ever, which is just before us, we are called to a renewed allegiance to the Creator. The issue here is not a vague concern for belief in some kind of god. The choice is between allegiance to a very personal God who created us because He loves us and who seeks a personal relationship with us, on the one hand, and allegiance to a humanly invented god and to human institutions and suppositions, of which evolutionary theory is just another pernicious manifestation, on the other. The issues are profound, and they lead either to eternal life or eternal death.

For many people, the issues regarding the seventh-day Sabbath are not clear now, but the book of Revelation implies that one day events will bring this choice into sharp focus. At that time, the decision whether or not to observe the seventh-day Sabbath will not be an arbitrary choice of a day, but a choice of whom we will worship. Will we choose to have a personal love relationship that will result in allegiance to our Creator God, or will we choose to cast our lot in with an apostate and corrupted human institution that demands our worship?[6]

The choice at the end of time will not be one of atheism versus worship of God. Atheism is already losing credibility,[7] and when Satan appears as an angel of light who performs miracles, atheism will be dead. The issue that remains will be whether or not we will choose commitment to the Bible as the foundational, divine source of truth, or we will choose (among other things) a soft version of Christianity that mixes a little of the Bible with a strong dose of the secular worldview, which, for many people, will include theistic evolution.

The division of Christianity into these two camps is already well under way. Even though Christians who sit in their church pews may not agree with them, most Christian theologians and other Christian scholars are moving enthusiastically to theistic evolution, and their denominational allegiances are being decided in favor of theistic evolution.

CHOOSE YOU THIS DAY

The paths are fundamentally different and end at entirely different destinations.

	What We Trust	
Human Reasoning		God
Scientific Findings	**Primary Evidence**	The Bible
Theistic Evolution	**Origin and Development of All Life-Forms**	Literal Creation
???	**Relationship to Sabbath**	Upholds Seventh-day Sabbath

The Church, the Body of Christ

An exception is the Seventh-day Adventist Church, even though some have a strong desire to change this position and to make our church more "modern," or "postmodern," and more compatible with what is, outside of our church, the majority view. But why should we change our doctrine to make it easier to evangelize people when doing so means surrendering the belief system and the commission God has given us?

We probably can't fully grasp the significance of this challenge unless we have a personal friendship with our Creator. Christianity is based on personal relationships with a very personal God. We follow Him because of love and trust, not because He demands it of us, or merely because we have a habit of going to church.

ENDNOTES

1. See, e.g., M. Moore, *The Case for the Investigative Judgment: Its Biblical Foundation* (Nampa, Idaho: Pacific Press®, 2010).

2. R. Chambers, *Vestiges of the Natural History of Creation* (London: John Churchill, 1844).

3. Exod. 20:8–11.

4. Rev. 14:7, NKJV.

5. See J. Paulien, "Revisiting the Sabbath in the Book of Revelation," *Journal of the Adventist Theological Society* 9 (1998): 179–198; and J. T. Baldwin, "Revelation 14:7: An Angel's Worldview," in *Creation, Catastrophe, and Calvary,* ed. J. T. Baldwin (Hagerstown, Md.: Review and Herald®, 2000), 19–39.

6. Rev. 13; 14. White, *The Great Controversy,* 604, 605.

7. McGrath, *The Twilight of Atheism.*

CHAPTER 12

THE SCIENTIFIC TURN: BIOLOGICAL EVOLUTION

In this chapter we discuss scientific evidence pertinent to the conflict between creation and evolution. We haven't provided a comprehensive examination of the evidence here, but we have included enough to illustrate the most significant issues and scientific trends. If you're not interested in these, you may wish to skip this section and go to the conclusion in chapter 15. For those who want more depth than the limited material we've included here provides, we have supplied references at the end of this book.

In the nineteenth century, Charles Darwin and his contemporaries put together the core of the modern theory of evolution. In Darwin's era, virtually nothing was known about molecular biology or about DNA and mutations. Darwin proposed that through generation after generation of organisms, slight variations would show up. As he considered the implications of those variations, he realized that some of them would make the animals that had them better suited to survive in their environments, while others would decrease their ability to survive. That realization led to the logical conclusion that the better-adapted organisms would live longer and produce more offspring than would the more poorly adapted organisms Thus, the more helpful variations would tend to survive and increase with the organisms they aided. Darwin called this process "natural selection," and he concluded that it was this process, acting upon generation after generation of living organisms through long periods of time, that resulted in the evolution of all types of plants and animals.

Philosophical trends already at work in the nineteenth century, combined with Darwin's careful maneuvering in the academic world of the sciences, prepared the way for acceptance of this theory.[1] Most nineteenth-century scientists weren't convinced that natural selection was powerful enough to explain all the forms of life that this world contains, but the mass of evidence Darwin presented in support of his theory—from fossils, observations of variation and selection in domestic animals, and biogeography—convinced many scientists that life could have arisen and developed without a creator.[2]

The laws of genetics that Gregor Mendel had discovered in the 1860s through extensive research were rediscovered in the early twentieth century, leading to great growth in the understanding of genetics. Further developments in the field of genetics clarified the power of natural selection. In the 1930s and 1940s, a group of biologists, paleontologists, and mathematicians combined what was then known about genetics, fossils, anatomy, natural selection, and the mathematical analysis of genetic changes in populations of organisms. The more advanced and sophisticated version of evolution that these scientists developed became known as the neo-Darwinian theory of evolution, or the neo-Darwinian synthesis.[3] At that point, most biologists considered Darwin's process of natural selection as the driving force in evolution, and neo-Darwinism was regarded as the theory that could explain all we need to know about the evolution of simple organisms into the extraordinarily widespread and diverse biological world we see around us.

In the 1950s, two developments added to the growing confidence in evolution. One was the description by Watson and Crick of the structure of DNA, which increased our understanding of how DNA functions as the source of genetic information in all organisms. This discovery was a significant addition to the neo-Darwinian theory.[4] Miller and Urey's experiments also showed that natural processes could make amino acids (the components of proteins) in the conditions presumed to exist on the primitive earth. In the eyes of many scientists, this made the naturalistic origin of life more plausible.[5] God now seemed truly to be unnecessary.

Scientists then envisioned the chance formation of one-celled organisms in a primordial chemical soup to be a relatively simple matter. These primitive organisms, then, were the material on which evolution could work, enabling the neo-Darwinian processes of random mutation and natural selection to produce increasingly complex plants and animals. The mutations are random in the sense that the mutation process doesn't know what the organism needs. But ultimately, the process isn't really random because natural selection tips the scale in favor of the survival of beneficial mutations and against the survival of harmful mutations. This is the process that, it was said, added improvement to improvement and thus produced the most complex creature of all—humans. There was enthusiastic confidence that this fully naturalistic process could satisfactorily explain biological origins and the evolution of life-forms with increasing variety and sophistication of form and function.

The word *evolution* has a variety of meanings, and we should avoid confusing them. Changes in life-forms, such as the development of resistance to antibiotics in bacteria and the adaptation of mice to different environments by changes in the color of their fur, are also called evolution. These microevolutionary processes of adaptation and the development of new species are not contrary to biblical creation and are supported by a lot of evidence.[6] Creationists' objections to the theory of evolution have to do primarily with large-scale evolution—for instance, the evolution of worms, reptiles, and humans from a common ancestor.

Evolution and the fossil record

The theory of large-scale evolution uses the fossil record as a history book that documents the story of the evolution of increasingly more complex organisms through deep time (many millions of years). This history book begins with marine invertebrates, which are preserved in Cambrian rocks. From that beginning, the passage of time is recorded in the rock layers stacked on top of the Cambrian layer—each successive layer containing fossils of new, more complex life-forms. Fish are found quite early in the record, then amphibians, and later, reptiles, which are followed by birds and mammals, with humans being one of the last types to show up as fossils. The order in which these animal groups appear in the fossil record fits the theory of evolution quite well.[7]

However, there is a problem in the fossil record that Darwin agonized over because he realized it could compromise his theory. The problem is that, in most cases, each group of organisms appears as fossils *without a series of intermediate forms showing how they evolved from their supposed ancestors.*[8] This is still a serious problem for evolution, although some vertebrate fossils have been found that can be interpreted as filling evolutionary gaps between living vertebrate groups.

Creationists have alternative explanations of most of these presumed evolutionary links, but a few are quite puzzling. We don't have the answers for all the questions, but that's OK. No one has the answers to all the questions about unobservable ancient history.

Cracks in the theory

Confidence that evolution will triumph over creationist ideas has increased, and this theory is universally proclaimed in textbooks, popular media, public schools, and now often in Christian pulpits too. And those who disagree are commonly portrayed as ignorant and poorly educated. This confidence results as much or more from a deepening commitment to the philosophy of naturalism than from the accumulation of more solid evidence, although many scientists proclaim that the evidence is overwhelming.

In reality, there are cracks in the naturalistic edifice, and they are growing. Those holding the naturalistic worldview are attempting to fill the cracks with many eloquent words; but those looking on from the outside of naturalism can see that the plaster isn't sticking, and the cracks are becoming more obvious.

One of the deepest cracks runs through the attempts to explain the origin of life. After the publication of Miller and Urey's experiments, it was enthusiastically proclaimed that we would soon know how life arose independent of any intelligent creator. Since then, more careful thinking and experiments have shown that the Miller and Urey scenario wasn't realistic. However, the origin of life by natural processes, with complex biological molecules forming and gradually accumulating to become the first living cells, is still textbook orthodoxy. Those holding to naturalism must believe it happened that way. However, a few scientists, even some bona fide naturalists, admit that we don't have any idea how life arose.[9]

Intelligent Design

As a result of some scientists' awareness of the cracks in naturalistic theory, a movement began during the 1980s that called attention to the need for better explanations. This Intelligent Design movement (ID) was begun by a highly qualified group of scientists and philosophers led by Phillip Johnson, a law professor at Berkeley. The ID movement emphasizes that the origin of life can be explained only as the work of an intelligent agent.[10]

Some conservative Christians are critical of ID because ID proponents don't mention the Christian God as the creative agent and don't address questions of the fossil record or of the evolution of life through time. We suggest that these criticisms are missing something significant about ID. The ID movement has limited itself to one issue of critical importance—the essentiality of a designer or creator to the origin of life. This is a matter of science as well as of philosophy and theology. That is, the scientific evidence we have for the beginning of life is best explained by design, and there are valid reasons for believing the origin of life cannot be explained without that designer or creator. But science can't determine who the designer is, and so ID leaves that determination to others (although some ID leaders are young-life-on-earth creationists).

By limiting itself to the one central issue that science can address, ID is working toward filtering the unnecessary and damaging philosophical assumptions of naturalism out of science. Increasing people's awareness of the difference between objective science and naturalistic assumptions is a necessary first step toward opening minds to the realization that an unbiased study of origins concludes that there must have been a designer. Those who have made the study of ID their concern have a full plate. They have to leave the next step—demonstration that God is that designer and that His Word is a reliable record of the history of life—up to others, such as ourselves.

Two components

Science has helped us recognize the amazing laws of chemistry and physics that God uses to operate His universe. If we push a boulder off a cliff, gravity will determine the outcome. No intelligent thought is required by anyone to make the consequences of this action consistent with those of other similar actions.

What then is so unique about life? Don't we operate within the same laws as the rest of the universe?

Yes—but only up to a point. Books are made of two very different components, one being the physical paper and ink, or, more recently, the screen and electrons, that bear the letters books contain; and the other being information—the meaning carried by the sequences of letters that form words and sentences. There is no law that specifies the order in which the letters are placed on the paper. The order of the letters is determined by ideas, by information; and ideas and information are the province of intelligent minds. Information originates only in intelligence.

Like books, life is comprised of two components: physical molecules and the information contained in the sequences of those molecules. Simple biological molecules, like amino acids, will form by the unaided action of chemical laws. But amino acids by themselves don't make anything alive. These simple molecules, and many others, must be arranged in the proper sequence in order to function properly. The sequence of amino acids in a protein is controlled by the sequence of another kind of simple molecules—nucleotides—also found in DNA. These amino acids and nucleotides are like bricks. Bricks alone won't make a palace; there must also be an engineer and a blueprint. And just as no natural law sets the sequences of letters and words on this page, no natural law sets the sequences of amino acids and nucleotides in the living cells that make up our bodies. All these sequences of molecules contain and communicate information that is directly comparable to the information contained and communicated in the sequences of letters in a book or in the letters and lines on a blueprint.

Crystals can be very beautiful, but they are simple, nonliving structures composed of a very repetitive sequence of a few elements. Their law-governed chemical composition can be represented by a sequence of letters, such as AFR AFR AFR AFR. In contrast, biological molecules are extremely complex. For example, there are thousands of types of proteins in every cell, and each type of protein is composed of thousands of subunits that must be in the right sequence for the protein to do its job. Just as the sequence of letters in the phrase "God loves you" conveys information, so do the sequences of molecules that make up the proteins that enable the living cell to perform its function. That's why crystals and living cells are radically different things.

Life exists because every life-form contains a massive

amount of information recorded in an incredibly complex and wonderful instruction book inside its cells—DNA.[11] It has been repeatedly demonstrated that there is no adequate explanation for such information other than that an intelligent "inventor"—in this case, God—put it there. The only alternative is pure chance, and the probability of all that information appearing in a cell spontaneously is so remote as to render this alternative a dead end. Mainline science denies that such complexity demands a Creator, but if we open our minds and think about it carefully, that denial doesn't ring true.

The ID movement is drawing attention to the distinction between information, on one hand, and law-governed phenomena, on the other. This movement is having an influence, opening the minds of those who are willing to see beyond modern, dogmatic naturalism, which they see that science doesn't need.

Molecular biology

Next, there's the crucial issue of the presumed large-scale evolution of life-forms—the progression from bacteria to worms and other invertebrates, and then from those creatures to fish, amphibians, reptiles, and mammals, and, finally, to humans. The structures, physiology, and brain functions of each life-form are governed by information in DNA. Each step in the proposed evolutionary sequence requires a large amount of new DNA information. The origin of the first simple life-forms and the unguided evolution of more complex life-forms, such as starfish, reptiles, and humans, all require

the origination of volumes of new biological information. Are random mutations and natural selection up to the task? Mainline science insists Yes, but that answer depends upon assumptions. Here we also find the cracks becoming wider—largely because of advances in molecular biology.

Darwin and his contemporaries had no idea how complex a living cell is. The scientists who put together the neo-Darwinian synthesis in the 1940s also knew relatively little about the nature of life. In their day, almost all the modern discoveries in molecular biology still lay in the future. Unfortunately, their view of life's origins, based on naturalistic theories, became entrenched in the scientific mind-set before scientists knew enough to make an objective evaluation of those theories. And since that approach has become deeply embedded in the thinking of an entire community, changing it is difficult.

More than a decade ago, at an annual meeting of the Society of Vertebrate Paleontologists, I listened to a presentation by a prominent evolutionary scientist in which he said that the neo-Darwinian synthesis needs to be redone, and "this time we aren't going to blow it." At the time, I wondered what he meant. Only now is the meaning finally becoming evident. Over the past several decades, molecular biology research has revealed increasing levels of sophistication in the operation of every cell in our bodies. King David marveled that we are so "fearfully and wonderfully made,"[12] and he knew only the most basic functioning of this marvelous machine, the living body. How he would marvel now!

Research has revealed that the cell's mechanisms for correcting mistakes in the duplication of DNA are vastly more precise than we had previously thought. And it is also now known that cells have many sensors that monitor their environment, gathering information that enables the cells to make needed alterations in their functioning. So, the DNA's control of the cells is not an automatic, one-way operation. Those environmental sensors provide feedback that can alter how the information in DNA is interpreted in the making and the operation of an organism.

In fact, the environment that we grow up in even makes what are called "epigenetic" changes in how the DNA is interpreted. These epigenetic changes don't alter the DNA, but they do influence how that DNA blueprint is interpreted, changing the offspring of those organisms. Those changes may be passed down for several generations. And if the environment returns to what it was originally, the organisms can go back to interpreting the information in the DNA in the original way.

In other words, because of epigenetics, the conditions in which a baby is born and raised can affect it and its offspring negatively or positively for several generations. This makes one think of the biblical statement, "He punishes the children for the sin of the fathers to the third and fourth generation."[13] It seems that He who inspired the Bible writers knew something about genetics!

One eminent evolutionary biologist involved in these discoveries describes the genetic system as doing what he calls "natural genetic engineering."[14] He points out that cells and organisms don't passively carry out fixed genetic instructions. Instead, they assertively use environmental information from their sensors to determine the most effective way to use the information in DNA. The genetic system "decides" what modifications will best serve the organism of which it is a part.

This same author states that these new discoveries about the genetic system leave no room for the random mutations proposed by Darwinian theory. This author is not a creationist; he is clearly committed to the evolution of life through deep time. However, the evidence has convinced him that this must happen through some mechanism other than the random mutations cited in the conventional Darwinian theory. When more traditional evolutionists, believers in Darwinian random mutation and natural selection, criticize him—and they do—he responds that "their position is philosophical, not scientific, nor is it based on empirical observations."[15] He also admits that he has no idea how this genetic system evolved. Even scientists who don't believe in Creation, if they're open to the evidence, can see that the sophistication of a living cell is mind-boggling!

There is much more that we could say about the difficulties the theory of evolution faces because of advances in molecular biology, molecular genetics, the human genome project and its spin-offs, and careful analysis of population genetics.[16] We predict these difficult challenges to large-scale evolution will multiply. The cracks in this part of the naturalistic worldview are growing wider and more menacing. Perhaps this is why the more vocal opponents of creationism are becoming increasingly abrasive and unreasonable.[17]

The fact that the theory of evolution is facing increasingly difficult challenges doesn't mean that creationists have answers for all the challenges creationism faces. We don't know how to explain some features of the fossil record, and many things in nature are so evil that they are hard to explain, even though we recognize that the work of the enemy, Satan, lies behind them.

However, we think geology poses questions that are even more challenging than those posed by biology. We turn now to that topic.

ENDNOTES

1. P. J. Bowler, *Charles Darwin: The Man and His Influence* (New York: Cambridge University Press, 1990).

2. J. P. Moreland, *Christianity and the Nature of Science* (Grand Rapids, Mich.: Baker Books, 1989); R. Numbers, *The Creationists* (New York: A. A. Knopf, 1992); E. Mayr, "The Modern Evolutionary Theory," *Journal of Mammalogy* 77 (1996): 1–7.

3. See the works cited in the previous endnote.

4. J. D. Watson and F. H. C. Crick, "Molecular Structure of Nucleic Acids," *Nature* 171, no. 4356 (April 25, 1953): 737, 738.

5. S. L. Miller, "Production of Amino Acids Under Possible Primitive Earth Conditions," *Science* 117, no. 3046 (May 1953): 528; S. L. Miller and H. C. Urey, "Organic Compound Synthesis on the Primitive Earth," *Science* 130, no. 3370 (July 1959): 245.

6. When microevolution results in small changes that keep two

populations of plants or animals from interbreeding, these two populations are considered, by definition, to be two differing species. This process is easily within the types of change that have occurred within created groups. There are approximately one thousand species of rats and mice, and they illustrate this process of speciation since creation.

7. Brand, *Faith, Reason, and Earth History,* 236–240, 271–274.

8. S. J. Gould and N. Eldredge, "Punctuated Equilibria: The Tempo and Mode of Evolution Reconsidered," *Paleobiology* 3 (1972): 115–151.

9. J. Shapiro, *Evolution: A View From the 21st Century* (Upper Saddle River, N.J.: FT Press, 2011), 125; F. H. C. Crick and L. E. Orgel, "Directed Panspermia," *Icarus* 19 (1973): 341–346.

10. P. E. Johnson, *Darwin on Trial* (Downers Grove, Ill.: InterVarsity Press, 1991); P. E. Johnson, *Reason in the Balance* (Downers Grove, Ill.: InterVarsity Press, 1995); Behe, *Darwin's Black Box;* P. E. Johnson, *Defeating Darwinism by Opening Minds* (Downers Grove, Ill.: InterVarsity Press, 1997); W. A. Dembski, *Intelligent Design* (Downers Grove, Ill.: InterVarsity Press, 1999); P. E. Johnson, *The Wedge of Truth* (Downers Grove, Ill.: InterVarsity Press, 2000); W. A. Dembski, *No Free Lunch* (Lanham, Md.: Rowman & Littlefield, 2002); M. J. Behe, *The Edge of Evolution* (New York: Free Press, 2007); Meyer, *Signature in the Cell.*

11. See the works cited in the previous endnote.

12. Ps. 139:14.

13. Num. 14:18, NIV; see also Exod. 20:5.

14. Shapiro, *Evolution: A View From the 21st Century.*

15. Ibid., 55, 56.

16. J. C. Sanford, *Genetic Entropy and the Mystery of the Genome,* 3rd ed. (Waterloo, N.Y.: FMS Publications, 2008).

17. The following are some recent examples from online discussions of evolution and from statements made publicly at national geology conferences: If there are more creationists, modern medicine and modern technology will end. University faculty shouldn't give recommendations for pre-med students if those students believe in Creation, because they can't be good doctors. It isn't possible to be a scientist and a creationist. Creationists flimflam the public with their ideas. Creationism isn't scientific. Teaching creationism is hazardous to our security, society, and future. If you reject evolution, then agriculture, biodiversity, and conservation make no sense. Because of what creationism is doing in the USA, by 2050 the USA will no longer hold first place in science; China, Japan, and India will be ahead of it.

These verbal slams remind me of the story of a preacher who wrote in the margin of his sermon notes, "Argument weak, shout louder"!

CHAPTER 13

GEOLOGICAL HISTORY

To understand how radiometric dating works, think of an hourglass that empties in one hour. The ratio of the amount of sand in the top of the hourglass to the amount of sand in the bottom tells how much time has passed since it was last turned over.

Some chemical elements, such as carbon and potassium, occur in more than one form, more than one isotope, and some of those isotopes are unstable. Unstable isotopes (the parent isotopes) "decay," becoming more stable isotopes (the daughter isotopes) at a regular, measurable rate, just as sand flows from the top to the bottom of the hourglass at a regular, measurable rate. Geologists start with, for instance, a rock containing an element that has those unstable parent isotopes. The time required for half of the parent isotopes of that particular element to decay into daughter isotopes is called the "half-life" of that element. Scientists have measured the half-life of the various radioactive elements, so they can determine the age of the rocks that contain those radioactive isotopes.

Here's how they do it. Let's say we have a rock sample we want to date using the potassium-argon method. The story of this rock sample began in the earth, when it was a semiliquid magma. During that time, some of its potassium-40 (the parent isotope) decayed, becoming a gas: argon-40 (the daughter isotope). Then the magma came up through an opening in the earth's crust to form a layer of new volcanic rock.

At that time, our rock sample had an age corresponding to the length of time it was in the earth. But we don't want to know that age. Instead, we want to know how long ago it came to the surface and formed the new rock layer. We assume that when it came to the surface, it lost all its argon-40; so we set the clock back to zero—in effect, turning the hourglass over to restart it. Then we measure what percentage of the remaining potassium-40 has changed to its daughter product, argon-40, and calculate its age. Other unstable elements don't produce daughter products that are gases, so they don't lose their daughter product. For those elements, a mathematical method is used to determine how much of the daughter isotope was present when it formed a new rock layer, and how much daughter isotope formed during the time we wish to measure, when the rock was at the surface of the earth.

The ratio of the amount of original or parent isotope to the amount of daughter isotope is used to calculate the age of the new rock layer. The instrument that measures the amounts of these isotopes that remain can't directly measure the age in years. It determines only the ratio of the parent isotope to the daughter isotope (how much sand is still in the top of the glass). The researcher makes some assumptions and then calculates the age. When our lab instrument analyzes many rock samples, it gives a ratio for each sample.

These ratios change in a regular pattern when the samples are taken from the rock layers that range from the bottom to the top of the geological column. The ratios don't always come out as expected, but generally they do show a consistent, predictable relationship to the position of the sample in the geological column. In other words, when ages are calculated from the ratios, the rocks at the bottom of the column are oldest, and the ratios indicate progressively younger ages as the samples approach the top of the geological column (see the geological-column diagram on page 58). From this we can conclude that these ratios do mean something. They give at least a relative age for the rocks; they distinguish older rocks from younger rocks. What we want to know now is whether they also give accurate ages in years.

What caused those ratios to be in that pattern? If the rock layers were there for many millions of years, the passage of time would produce that sequence of ratios. But if the fossil record and the sedimentary rocks (Cambrian to Recent) in which it was enclosed are only a few thousand years old, some other factors caused that sequence of ratios to form as it has.[1] Scientists who have accepted the naturalistic worldview and base their conclusions on it will reject that suggestion totally, but if there is evidence that challenges the great age of the fossil-bearing rocks, the suggestion of other factors affecting radiometric ratios (altering the decay process) should not be arbitrarily rejected. We weren't there to see what was happening to the rocks during that time, so we can't be sure.

Evidence against long ages

The God who inspired (informed) the Bible writers knew about epigenetics and about salvation through Jesus. Some of us think that what we know of Him justifies believing that He also knows the true age of the fossils and the sediments that enclose them. We have other relevant evidence as well.

Remember our story about Lassie and the five layers of mud? (See chapter 6.) Suppose now that three layers were deposited in quick succession, and then one hundred years passed before a fourth flood deposited a layer. Is it likely that the first three layers would remain undisturbed all that time? No, that isn't likely. No doubt erosion would carve away parts of the layers and cut little valleys through what was left. And if portions of the layers did remain the full one hundred years, the activities of earthworms, insects, gophers, mice, and plant roots would destroy any clear boundaries between the layers. So, if we dug down through the layers, it would be difficult or even impossible for us to see just how many layers there were originally.

We see these processes happening today when sedimentary layers form under water. Numerous little creatures churn up the sediment and destroy evidence of the boundaries. It seems we could expect that the same processes would alter the larger and more numerous sedimentary layers in the geological column if, as most scientists claim, they were deposited gradually through millions of years.

When we examine the layers in the geological column, we do find evidence of erosion as well as fossil animal burrows in the sediment. *But there is not nearly enough of either to account for such long time periods.* Far too much of the geological record occurs as distinct, very persistent layers extending laterally for many miles without the irregular, eroded surfaces that we see forming on the earth today. In many places, sedimentary layers sitting one above the other give dates indicating that many millions of years—even up to 150 million years—passed between the depositing of adjacent layers—yet the lower layer, the one that has lain exposed all that time, often has little evidence of erosion. The geological processes we observe on earth today, the laws of physics and chemistry, and the modern biological processes we're acquainted with tell us that to think that layers of mud or sand or even rock could stand uncovered for time spans of that length without any erosion taking place is unrealistic.[2]

As you study those many distinct layers of rock, think about the worms and gophers that churn up the layers of mud in our backyard. Similar animal and plant activities while the sediment was still soft should have destroyed any distinct layering in the geological record. Yes, we do find fossil animal burrows, but typically not enough to obscure the distinct layering. These paraconformities are so typical of the geological record that they pose a strong challenge to the theory of long ages of time. It seems apparent that the rock layers were deposited too rapidly for them to be as churned up and eroded as we would expect them to be if they were there for the time radioactive dating seems to suggest.

ENDNOTES

1. Since the Precambrian rocks could have been created some time before the Creation event described in Genesis (see chapter 4), we are speaking in this section only about the rocks in which complex fossils were buried—the rocks and fossils formed from the Cambrian era to the present. The Bible doesn't help us determine how old most Precambrian rocks are.
2. Roth, "Those Gaps in the Sedimentary Layers," 75–92, http://www.grisda.org/origins/15075.htm.

CHAPTER 14

GEOLOGICAL TIME AND SCIENTIFIC THINKING

The nineteenth-century lawyer and geologist Charles Lyell (1797–1875) wrote a book that turned the adolescent field of geology into an organized science.[1] Many of the geologists of that time and before believed the evidence showed that some or even many rock formations had been formed rapidly, as the result of catastrophic events. Lyell rejected these interpretations of earth's geology, insisting that all geological formations developed in the same way as we see them being developed today—very slowly and gradually, as rivers and streams deposit sediments. Lyell's views held sway for a century, and the concept of uniformitarianism became geological dogma. No explanations involving catastrophes were accepted.

But trouble was brewing. In the 1920s, a young, independent-thinking geologist who went by the name J. Harlen Bretz began to study a region in eastern Washington State that had unusual geological features.[2] The rock in that entire region was quite uniform; the whole region had been covered up to a depth of six thousand feet with very hard volcanic basalt. What made this region unusual was that the layer of basalt was eroded into a wild system of deep channels and canyons with strange surface topography. The area came to be called the Channeled Scablands.

Bretz and his students spent a number of summers doing research there, and Bretz saw abundant evidence that he could explain only as catastrophic erosion caused by an enormous amount of fast-moving water. Bretz published papers on his findings in geology journals, but his colleagues scorned his ideas. Suggestions that catastrophes caused geological features weren't welcome. Other geologists, most of whom had done little or no research in the Scablands themselves, presented theories of how the Scablands could have been shaped gradually by water or glacial ice during the Pleistocene glaciation.

On one occasion, Bretz was invited to present his conclusions at a gathering of prestigious geologists in Washington, D.C. He saw the event as an opportunity to make his case before this august group. After he spoke, other geologists also gave presentations, all of them sarcastically opposing Bretz's ideas. It was obvious the meeting had been a setup to humiliate Bretz—he faced a lynching because he questioned deeply held uniformitarian assumptions.[3]

But Bretz was made of stern stuff. Refusing to stop thinking for himself, he followed the evidence where it led him, even if it meant he had to buck the tide of Lyell's settled dogma. Eventually, the tide turned, and Bretz is now uniformly recognized as a hero—the one person who discovered what made the Scablands.

Catastrophism

Where did Bretz's flood come from? A part of a glacial ice sheet that extended from Canada into the United States blocked the lower end of a mountain valley in western Montana, near Missoula. (Creationists believe the "ice age" involved here wasn't hundreds of thousands or millions of years ago, but shortly after the biblical Flood.) This ice dam held back all the water that drained from a large area of the Rocky Mountains, forming what is now called Lake Missoula. This dam broke; and when it broke, it released five hundred cubic miles of water, which screamed across eastern Washington at fifty to seventy miles per hour, carving out the Channeled Scablands in a few days. This may have happened more than once.

Bretz's work turned the tide, breaking up the dogmatic rejection of theories that involved catastrophic geological events. Because of Bretz's persistence, geologists now recognize that catastrophic processes have helped shape our planet. Now, geologists even admit that the catastrophists of Lyell's time were better observers of geology than Lyell was.[4]

However, there is still a definite limit to how much catastrophism modern science is willing to accept. Naturalistic thinking still pervades science, and the theory of evolution still requires those many millions of years. Thus, even though geologists admit that there have been catastrophes, thinking this suggests that catastrophes played a role in shaping the earth's surface and that goes so far as to question the geological timescale still is not welcome. An overwhelming bias toward interpreting geological formations as forming over many millions of years still exists.

For example, a team of geologists recently studied three sandstone formations in Russia.[5] They analyzed the grain size and sedimentary structures in the sandstone and calculated the rate at which the sand must have been deposited to account for the sandstone's features. The evidence indicated the sandstone must have accumulated in 0.05 percent or less of the time indicated by the sandstone's radiometric age. Conventional geological thinking can't tolerate such a radical reduction in geological time, so the researchers decided there must have been many cycles of sand accumulating, eroding away, accumulating, and eroding away again. That would stretch the time involved and match the theory of evolution better. However, that interpretation requires many more episodes of erosion than are recorded in the rocks; thus, it is strictly an ad hoc hypothesis cobbled together solely to shoehorn what evidence there is into the conventional geology theory.

Unfortunately, this isn't an isolated situation—it's a common practice in geology. The time required to accumulate the amount of sediment needed to form a geological structure is often only one ten-thousandth to one one-hundred-thousandth or less of the time that radiometric studies indicate the structure has existed.[6]

Evolution and time

These examples of evidence and theory illustrate some

principles of truly *scientific* studies and of how a biblical scientist can relate to it all. Since we believe the Bible gives factual, trustworthy history, scientific concepts dependent upon the existence of life on earth for millions of years have to be wrong. And, closing those doors is actually helpful, because it simultaneously opens to us whole new areas that we can research (stage 2 research), and it increases the likelihood that we will make discoveries that others can't visualize because the boundaries of evolution narrow what they consider the possibilities to be. The research approach that benefits from the guidelines implicit in the Bible continues to make progress, answering questions and eliminating conflicts. We predict this process will continue to be successful.

We hope the progress that Bible-oriented research has made and the realization that questions remain have sparked your interest. But even biblically oriented research hasn't answered all our questions, including that of how long life has existed on this earth. So, we remind you also of the important role faith plays in carrying us beyond the unanswered questions.

Many Christians make the mistake of expecting to have answers to all their questions before they trust God's Word. Naturalistic scientists face plenty of serious unanswered questions about evolution, and they have faith that answers that support their theory will eventually be found. Should we have less faith?

When God spoke to Job after Job had lost so much, He didn't answer Job's questions. Instead, He showed Job how little he knew compared to what God knows.[7] Job didn't need to have all the answers; he needed to learn to trust God with his future.

Thinking that in our short lifetimes we can find answers to most, if not all, of the important questions is unrealistic. Like Job, we don't need to have all the answers. We just need to learn to trust God.

ENDNOTES

1. C. Lyell, *Principles of Geology,* 3 vols. (London: John Murray, 1830–1833).

2. J. Soennichsen, *Bretz's Flood* (Seattle, Wash.: Sasquatch Books, 2008). An excellent video on the Scablands geology is "Mystery of the Megaflood," *NOVA,* directed by Ben Fox (Boston: NOVA/WGBH Boston, 2005), DVD.

3. Soennichsen, *Bretz's Flood,* 194.

4. S. J. Gould, "Toward the Vindication of Punctuational Change," in *Catastrophes and Earth History: The New Uniformitarianism,* eds. W. A. Berggren and J. A. Van Couvering (Princeton, N.J.: Princeton University Press, 1984), 9–34.

5. G. Berthault, A. V. Lalomov, and M. A. Tugarova, "Reconstruction of Paleolithodynamic Formation Conditions of Cambrian-Ordovician Sandstones in the Northwestern Russian Platform," *Lithology and Mineral Resources* 46, no. 1 (2011): 60–70.

6. Ibid., 68.

7. Job 38:1–40:2.

Chapter 15

Conclusions

We face a decision. We must choose one of two alternatives: a literal, biblical creation or theistic evolution. And the choice we make is critically important. Theistic evolution denies the trustworthiness of Scripture and blames God for evil, denying that it resulted from human sin. It leaves us, then, with a God who is the author of pain and death. This is why we must understand the proper relationship between faith and science.

We could make a long list of past and present conflicts between science and the Bible—much longer than the list in this book. We could then group these conflicts by which stage they are currently in. Some are in stage 1, the conflict—and maybe confusion—stage. Others are in stage 2. They're still being studied, but are moving toward resolution. Still others are in stage 3, where diligent, honest Bible study and careful scientific research have resolved what seemed to be a genuine conflict, giving us new insights.

The real question is not whether science has proven the Bible to be false or whether we can prove our beliefs. Rather, it is where the various scientific challenges to the Bible are in the three-stage process that moves from conflict to resolution. We make this claim partly in faith, but partly also from the experience of observing this process for several decades, during which a number of these apparent conflicts moved through the process and reached stage 3.

Some conflicts, like the Galileo affair, have required considerable time and hindsight to reach stage 3. But as we gain experience in applying the process called the "Interface," we find that it becomes easier to recognize the approach that, combined with thorough research, is most likely to move the problem toward resolution. If we make the Bible our standard, it becomes the means of leading us toward new scientific findings. We don't test scientific interpretations directly with the Bible (see the figure on page 20), but the Bible provides the trustworthy foundation that helps us recognize scientific assertions that need further examination.

When we encounter a seeming conflict between Scripture and science, the journey from stage 1 to stage 3 begins as we direct our attention to the aspect of scientific interpretation that needs reexamination. We must study the Bible carefully to be sure that we haven't misunderstood its message, and we must analyze the science, looking for alternate hypotheses and for predictions we can test with scientific research (stage 2). This is a challenging process, which is to be expected when we're exploring new territory. When a new explanation for the data is found, and it stands up to critical scrutiny both from the angle of the Bible and from that of science, we have reached stage 3.

Science often corrects inadequate scientific ideas and does

so without help from Scripture, but the process described here can give us an advantage and speed up the process considerably. This applies primarily to the study of origins, which is especially affected by the dominant scientific philosophy of naturalism because naturalism doesn't accept any explanations that depend on or even imply divine involvement in earth history. If we allow the Bible to open our eyes to new ideas, we can have the advantage of seeing things in nature that others don't see because of their naturalistic bias. The Bible also opens our minds and hearts to the spiritual choice that we face.

The great controversy between Christ and Satan is, at this time in history, focusing in on the issues of the credibility of the Creator and the Creation story in Genesis. That's why the choice we face is a crucial one—one that involves choosing between two different views of creation; views that have far-reaching implications regarding our belief in God; views that are rapidly dividing the Christian world into two camps.

Theistic Evolution	The Literal, Biblical Story of the Creation of Life
1. Life has evolved through millions of years.	1. All life-forms on earth were created during a literal seven-day Creation week a few thousand years ago.
2. Science is our standard.	
3. Human wisdom is sufficient.	2. The Bible is our standard.
4. God is responsible for evil.	3. We need the wisdom God has given in the Bible.
5. The Sabbath is essentially a weak, meaningless symbol.	4. Evil is the result of sin.
	5. The Bible Sabbath celebrates what God created—including all life forms on earth—during a literal, seven-day Creation week.

Science is an important human endeavor, but we can know what to believe and what to reject only if we've made the Bible our standard for evaluating stories of our origin, of the beginning of evil, and of the intervention of our great God. The choice we make will prepare us for this age's final events, when Jesus returns to rescue repentant sinners from this evil-ridden earth.

Do you know Jesus? Is He your best Friend—Someone whose word you trust no matter what comes? This is the crux of the matter.

GENERAL REFERENCES

For those who wish to study the scientific issues in more depth, we suggest the following books.

Bryan W. Ball, ed., *In the Beginning: Science and Scripture Confirm Creation* (Nampa, Idaho: Pacific Press®, 2012). Seventeen chapters by seventeen authors—Bible scholars and scientists—present reasons for belief in creation.

Leonard Brand with David C. Jarnes, *Beginnings* (Nampa, Idaho: Pacific Press®, 2006). Aimed at the layperson, this book on creation and evolution is sometimes used as a secondary-school reference or text.

Leonard R. Brand, *Faith, Reason, and Earth History,* 2nd ed. (Berrien Springs, Mich.: Andrews University Press, 2009). This book provides a systematic presentation of the topics having to do with the philosophy of science, faith and science, theories of biological origins, and geological history. Written by a creationist, it compares creationist and non-creationist views. An educated layperson can understand this book, which is often used as a textbook.

L. James Gibson and Humberto M. Rasi, eds., *Understanding Creation* (Nampa, Idaho: Pacific Press®, 2011). Comprising twenty chapters on selected topics by twenty authors, this book is written in nontechnical language.

Ariel Roth, *Origins: Linking Science and Scripture* (Hagerstown, Md.: Review and Herald®, 1998). This book presents another creationist scientist and author's views on similar topics to Brand's *Faith, Reason, and Earth History*.